Eyewitness
DOG

Great Dane puppies

Bloodhound

Red fox

Skeleton of
maned wolf

Australian silky terrier

Shampooed
poodle

Eyewitness
DOG

Bronze Anubis,
c. 600 BCE–CE 300

Australian terrier

Two Salukis

Written by
JULIET CLUTTON-BROCK

English setter

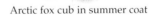

Arctic fox cub in summer coat

DK Publishing, Inc.

Beagle
tracking

Long-haired and miniature wire-haired dachshunds

Raccoon dog in winter coat

Skull of fennec fox

DK

LONDON, NEW YORK, MELBOURNE,
MUNICH, and DELHI

Project editor Marion Dent
Art editor Jutta Kaiser-Atcherley
Senior editor Helen Parker
Senior art editor Julia Harris
Production Louise Barratt
Picture research Cynthia Hole
Special photography Jerry Young,
Alan Hills of the British Museum,
Colin Keates of the Natural History Museum

REVISED EDITION
Managing editors Linda Esposito, Andrew Macintyre
Managing art editor Jane Thomas
Senior editor David John
Project art editor Joanne Little
Editor Sarah Phillips
Art editor Rebecca Johns
Production Luca Bazzoli
Picture research Harriet Mills
DTP designer Siu Yin Ho
Consultant Kim Bryan

U.S. editor Elizabeth Hester
Senior editor Beth Sutinis
Art editor Dirk Kaufman
U.S. production Chris Avgherinos
U.S. DTP designer Milos Orlovic

Cross-bred dog

This Eyewitness ® Guide has been conceived by Dorling Kindersley
Limited and Editions Gallimard

This edition published in the United States in 2004
by DK Publishing, Inc., 375 Hudson Street, New York, NY 10014

04 05 06 07 08 10 9 8 7 6 5 4 3 2 1

Copyright © 1991, © 2004 Dorling Kindersley Limited

A catalog record for this book is available from the
Library of Congress

ISBN 0-7566-0678-0 (HC) 0-7566-0677-2 (Library Binding)

Color reproduction by Colourscan, Singapore
Printed in China by Toppan Printing Co., (Shenzhen) Ltd

Discover more at
www.dk.com

Lurcher

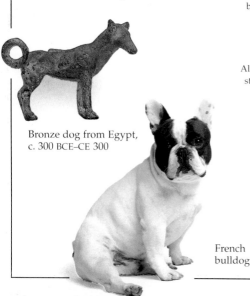

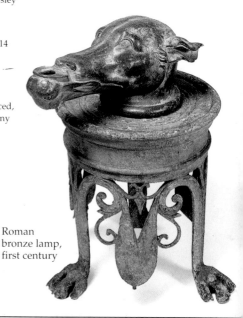

Bronze dog from Egypt,
c. 300 BCE–CE 300

French
bulldog

Roman
bronze lamp,
first century

Contents

Boxer

What is a dog?

PRAYING FOR PREY
St. Hubert, patron saint of hunters, is shown with his hounds by German painter Albrecht Dürer (1471–1528).

THE DOG FAMILY, called Canidae from the Latin *canis* meaning "dog," includes approximately 37 species of wolves, jackals, foxes, and wild and domestic dogs. All members of the dog family, or canids, are carnivores (meat eaters) and have special adaptations for hunting. Their teeth (pp. 8–9) are used for killing prey, chewing meat, and gnawing bones – and sometimes for fighting each other. Their highly developed senses of sight, sound, and smell (pp. 14–17) – with their large eyes, erect ears, and sensitive noses – mean they can track prey successfully, whether they are social or solitary hunters (pp. 18–19). All wild dogs, except for the South American bush dog (pp. 32–33), have long legs adapted for running fast in pursuit of prey. All canids are "digitigrade" (they walk on their toes) and have distinctive feet, with five claws on the front foot and four on the hind. In domestic dogs, there is sometimes an extra, fifth claw (dewclaw) on the hind foot. Wild dogs have long tails, and their dense fur is usually a solid color without spots or stripes (pp. 12–13). Canids mate once a year, and after two months' development in the womb, a litter of pups is born (pp. 20–21). Like all mammals, the mother suckles her young after they are born and cares for them for several months, with help from the rest of the family.

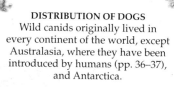

DISTRIBUTION OF DOGS
Wild canids originally lived in every continent of the world, except Australasia, where they have been introduced by humans (pp. 36–37), and Antarctica.

Coat is multicolored and distinctive

Ears are small, erect, and rounded

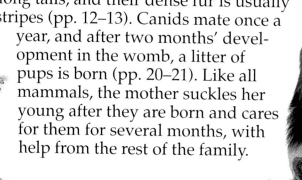

Golden jackal

THE JOVIAL JACKAL
There are four species of jackal (pp. 24–25) – the golden, the side-striped, the black-backed, and the Simien. All of the species live in Africa, but the golden also lives in parts of Europe and Asia. Jackals live and hunt in pairs and usually stay together for life.

Bushy tail, or brush

Red fox

RED SOLITAIRE
The red fox is a solitary hunter of rabbits and rodents. The fox is the only canid that does not hunt in a pack (pp. 28–29). The most characteristic part of the fox is its bushy tail.

DOGGIES OF ALL SORTS
Dogs have been bred in an amazing assortment of shapes, sizes, and colors. This painting shows just some of the 400 breeds of domestic dogs (pp. 48–61) in the world. All these breeds are descended from the wolf, which was first tamed by humans about 12,000 years ago (pp. 8–9).

WARM FEET
Of the many ways dogs have helped people, one of the more unusual ones was as a foot warmer for church congregations in the Middle Ages. Shown in this beautiful stained glass (right) are the biblical characters Tobias and Sarah – and their dog.

Teeth number the usual 42 (pp. 8–9), but first lower molars are small and flat – unlike other dogs' teeth

THE LARGEST CANID
The wolf (pp. 22–23) is the largest of all the wild canids. It lives and hunts in a family group, or pack, and is the most social (pp. 18–19) of all the carnivores. The wolf is the ancestor of all domestic dogs (pp. 48–61).

This wolf has thick gray fur, but the fur can vary from nearly pure white to red to brown or black

Gray wolf

AFRICAN HUNTER
The African hunting dog is a highly developed social carnivore (pp. 18–19) that hunts in family groups. These wild dogs live in the grasslands of Africa (pp. 26–27), but are in danger of extinction. Great numbers of them are being hunted and poisoned by farmers; they are also dying from disease, particularly canine distemper.

African hunting dog

Muzzle was heavy, and its teeth were very different from a dog's

Shorter hind legs give typical crouching position

Long, powerful front legs

This striped hyena is found in Africa and western Asia. Hyenas are hunters and scavengers; their powerful teeth can crush bones that even big cats are not able to chew.

The Tasmanian wolf looked similar to a dog, but it was a marsupial and unrelated to the dog family. It is now known only from stuffed specimens in museums.

Rounded ears

Thick, muscular base of tail could not wag like a dog's

What is not a dog?

Sometimes called dogs, the hyena, Tasmanian wolf, and prairie dog are not in the dog family. The three species of hyena, within the Hyaenidae family, are more closely related to cats. The Tasmanian wolf, or thylacine, now extinct, was a marsupial (pouched mammal) that lived in Australia, and the North American prairie dog is a rodent related to squirrels.

Prairie dogs are highly social rodents that live in communal burrows covering up to 160 acres.

Evolution of the dog family

THIRTY MILLION YEARS AGO, during the Oligocene period, the first doglike creature, *Cynodictis* (a mongoose-like animal with a long muzzle), appeared on Earth. It replaced the earlier widespread group of carnivores – the creodonts. All the earliest fossils of the dog family have been found in North America and date from this period. Another canid-like carnivore, *Tomarctus*, evolved during the Miocene period, about 24 million years ago. In turn, the genus *Canis* evolved, which gradually developed into *Canis lupus*, or the wolf, some 300,000 years ago. The first domestic dogs date from around 12,000 years ago. There were also creatures that looked similar to these dog ancestors, such as the hyaenodonts from the Oligocene, but they were not related to true hyenas, which are closer to the cat family. From ancestral carnivores like *Cynodictis*, the canids evolved into fast-running meat eaters that hunted prey on open grasslands, and most of today's living species have inherited this way of life.

BE SIRIUS
The brightest star in the sky is the Dog Star (Sirius) in the Canis Major constellation. Just as vast changes have taken place over millions of years in space, so the family of dogs has evolved over millions of years on Earth.

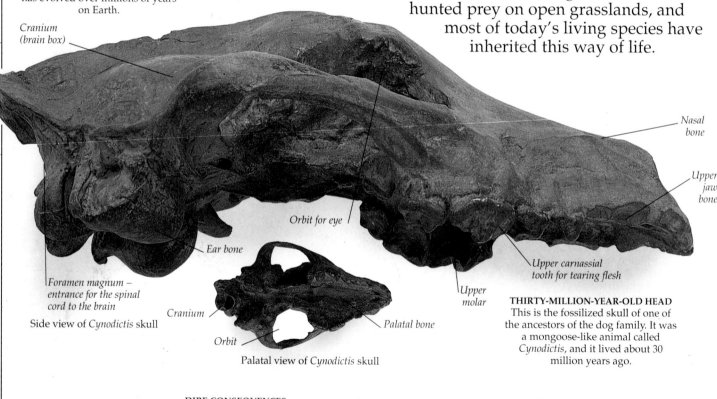

Cranium (brain box)

Nasal bone

Upper jaw bone

Orbit for eye

Ear bone

Upper carnassial tooth for tearing flesh

Foramen magnum – entrance for the spinal cord to the brain

Cranium

Upper molar

THIRTY-MILLION-YEAR-OLD HEAD
This is the fossilized skull of one of the ancestors of the dog family. It was a mongoose-like animal called *Cynodictis*, and it lived about 30 million years ago.

Side view of *Cynodictis* skull

Orbit

Palatal bone

Palatal view of *Cynodictis* skull

DIRE CONSEQUENCES
The extinct dire wolf (below) lived in California during the period of the Ice Ages. It was huge – much larger than any living wolf – and it preyed on the mammoth and other large Ice Age mammals.

Restoration of dire wolf

Reconstruction of a scene at the tar pits of La Brea near Los Angeles, showing dire wolves and a *Smilodon* attacking a mammoth (right)

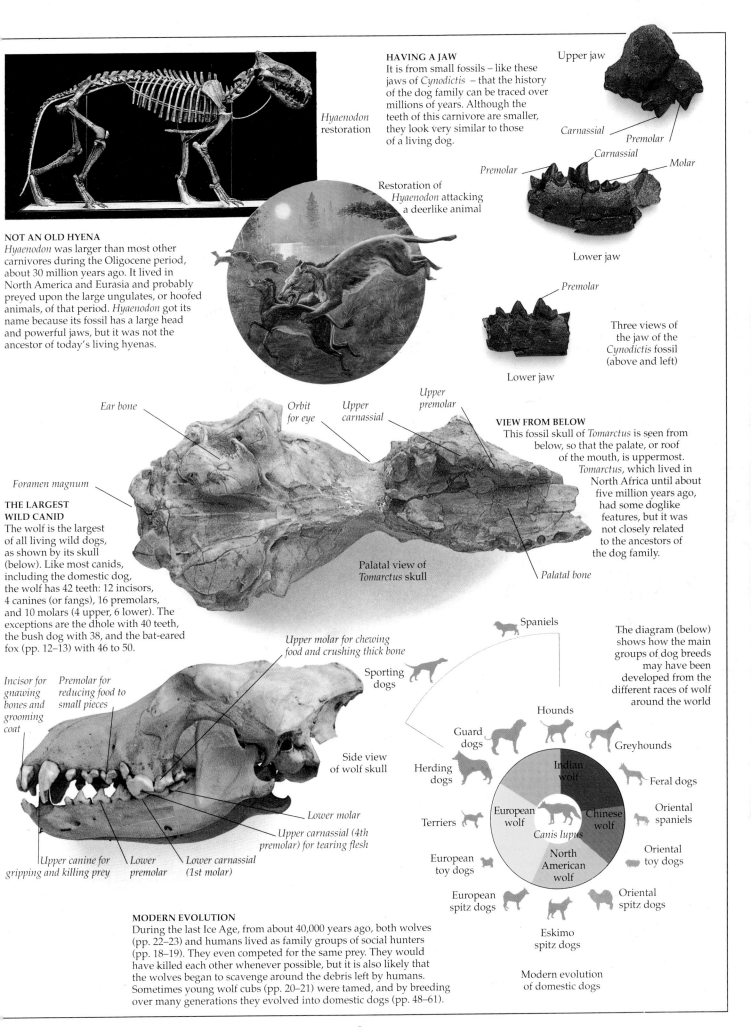

HAVING A JAW
It is from small fossils – like these jaws of *Cynodictis* – that the history of the dog family can be traced over millions of years. Although the teeth of this carnivore are smaller, they look very similar to those of a living dog.

Hyaenodon restoration

Upper jaw

Carnassial *Premolar*

Carnassial

Premolar *Molar*

Lower jaw

Restoration of *Hyaenodon* attacking a deerlike animal

NOT AN OLD HYENA
Hyaenodon was larger than most other carnivores during the Oligocene period, about 30 million years ago. It lived in North America and Eurasia and probably preyed upon the large ungulates, or hoofed animals, of that period. *Hyaenodon* got its name because its fossil has a large head and powerful jaws, but it was not the ancestor of today's living hyenas.

Premolar

Three views of the jaw of the *Cynodictis* fossil (above and left)

Lower jaw

Ear bone Orbit for eye Upper carnassial Upper premolar

Foramen magnum

VIEW FROM BELOW
This fossil skull of *Tomarctus* is seen from below, so that the palate, or roof of the mouth, is uppermost. *Tomarctus*, which lived in North Africa until about five million years ago, had some doglike features, but it was not closely related to the ancestors of the dog family.

THE LARGEST WILD CANID
The wolf is the largest of all living wild dogs, as shown by its skull (below). Like most canids, including the domestic dog, the wolf has 42 teeth: 12 incisors, 4 canines (or fangs), 16 premolars, and 10 molars (4 upper, 6 lower). The exceptions are the dhole with 40 teeth, the bush dog with 38, and the bat-eared fox (pp. 12–13) with 46 to 50.

Palatal view of *Tomarctus* skull

Palatal bone

Upper molar for chewing food and crushing thick bone

Spaniels

Sporting dogs

The diagram (below) shows how the main groups of dog breeds may have been developed from the different races of wolf around the world

Incisor for gnawing bones and grooming coat

Premolar for reducing food to small pieces

Hounds

Guard dogs

Greyhounds

Side view of wolf skull

Herding dogs

Indian wolf

Feral dogs

Lower molar

Terriers

European wolf

Canis lupus

Chinese wolf

Oriental spaniels

Upper carnassial (4th premolar) for tearing flesh

European toy dogs

North American wolf

Oriental toy dogs

Upper canine for gripping and killing prey

Lower premolar

Lower carnassial (1st molar)

European spitz dogs

Eskimo spitz dogs

Oriental spitz dogs

Modern evolution of domestic dogs

MODERN EVOLUTION
During the last Ice Age, from about 40,000 years ago, both wolves (pp. 22–23) and humans lived as family groups of social hunters (pp. 18–19). They even competed for the same prey. They would have killed each other whenever possible, but it is also likely that the wolves began to scavenge around the debris left by humans. Sometimes young wolf cubs (pp. 20–21) were tamed, and by breeding over many generations they evolved into domestic dogs (pp. 48–61).

Dogs' bones

THE SKELETON OF A MAMMAL provides the solid framework on which the rest of the body is built. The bones of the skull protect the brain, mouth, eyes, nose, and ears. The backbone supports the heart, lungs, and digestive system. The shoulder blade and hip girdle are the pivots that allow the limb bones to move. Attached to the ends of the bones are ligaments and tendons, which act like strong elastic to keep them joined together yet movable. Muscles are also attached to the bones in a complicated system that enables the body to move in all directions. Each bone in a canid's skeleton has characteristics that make it recognizable as belonging to a member of the dog family. Wolves, dogs (both wild and domestic), and foxes have long skulls and large teeth. The neck and the backbone are also relatively long, the ribs form a strong cage to protect the chest, and the long limb bones are adapted for fast running.

OLD MOTHER HUBBARD
This familiar nursery rhyme crone has no bones for her dog to chew (pp. 62–63) – "her cupboard is bare."

Skull of a wolf can always be recognized by the large size of the tearing, or carnassial, teeth

LARGE AS LIFE
Apart from some giant domestic dogs, the wolf (pp. 22–23) has the largest skeleton of all the animals in the dog family.

Arctic wolf

Neck vertebrae

Sternum

Elbow joint

Radius

Ulna

AFRICAN HUNTER
The African hunting dog (pp. 26–27) has very long legs in relation to the size of its body, so it is able to range over huge distances in search of prey.

African hunting dog

Skeleton of African hunting dog

Red fox

LITTLE RED
The red fox spends much of its time creeping under bushes and rocks. It has shorter legs in relation to the size of its body than the wolf does.

Radius

Ulna

Elbow joint

Tibia

Pelvis

Hock, or ankle joint

Skeleton of red fox

Lower jaw

Shoulder joint

Sternum

Metacarpal bone

Skeleton of Maltese dog

BALL OF FLUFF
This fluffy Maltese dog does not look at all like a wolf, but inside its skin the skeleton is just like that of a tiny wolf.

Round skull

Neck is short, but still has seven vertebrae

Maltese dog

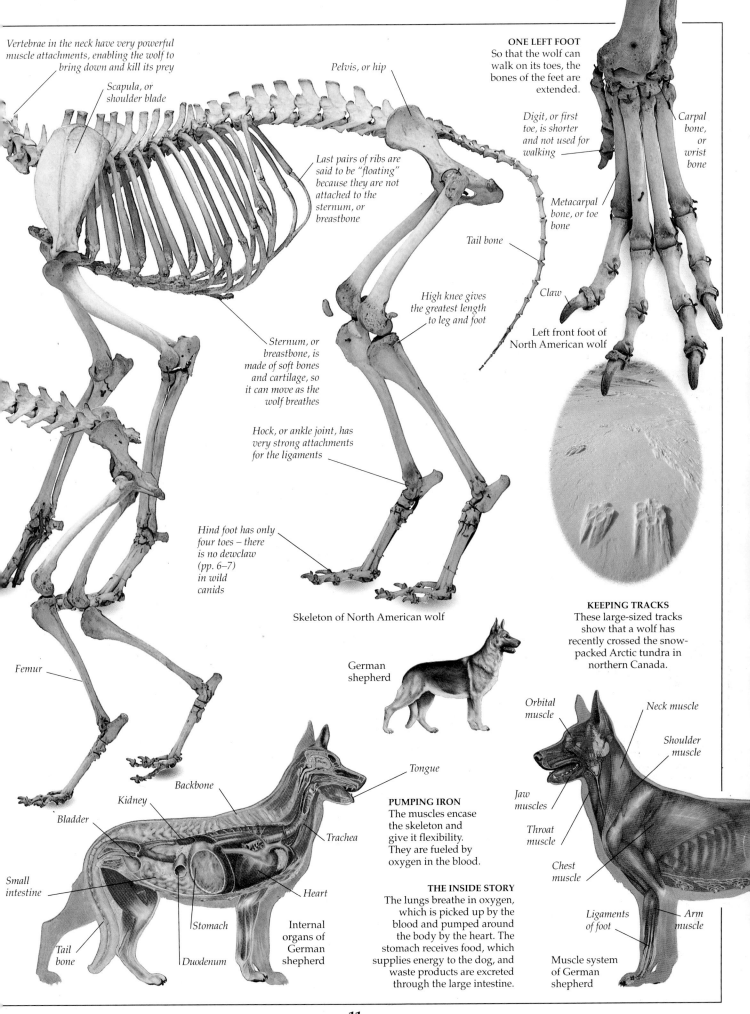

Vertebrae in the neck have very powerful muscle attachments, enabling the wolf to bring down and kill its prey

Scapula, or shoulder blade

Pelvis, or hip

ONE LEFT FOOT
So that the wolf can walk on its toes, the bones of the feet are extended.

Last pairs of ribs are said to be "floating" because they are not attached to the sternum, or breastbone

Digit, or first toe, is shorter and not used for walking

Carpal bone, or wrist bone

Metacarpal bone, or toe bone

Tail bone

High knee gives the greatest length to leg and foot

Claw

Sternum, or breastbone, is made of soft bones and cartilage, so it can move as the wolf breathes

Left front foot of North American wolf

Hock, or ankle joint, has very strong attachments for the ligaments

Hind foot has only four toes – there is no dewclaw (pp. 6–7) in wild canids

Femur

Skeleton of North American wolf

KEEPING TRACKS
These large-sized tracks show that a wolf has recently crossed the snow-packed Arctic tundra in northern Canada.

German shepherd

Orbital muscle

Neck muscle

Shoulder muscle

Tongue

Jaw muscles

Backbone

Kidney

PUMPING IRON
The muscles encase the skeleton and give it flexibility. They are fueled by oxygen in the blood.

Throat muscle

Bladder

Trachea

Chest muscle

THE INSIDE STORY
The lungs breathe in oxygen, which is picked up by the blood and pumped around the body by the heart. The stomach receives food, which supplies energy to the dog, and waste products are excreted through the large intestine.

Heart

Small intestine

Stomach

Internal organs of German shepherd

Ligaments of foot

Arm muscle

Tail bone

Duodenum

Muscle system of German shepherd

Coats, heads, and tails

A DOG'S FUR IS NECESSARY to keep the dog warm; its fur is denser in cold climates, and shorter in hot ones. It is composed of two layers: an undercoat of fine wool, usually of one color, and a top coat of longer, coarser hairs, called guard hairs, which have natural oils that make the coat waterproof. The top coat carries the brindled, or striped, pattern of the fur. The heads of all wild dogs look very much alike. Whether large like the wolf or small like the bat-eared fox, all wild canids have long heads with erect ears, and teeth set in a line along straight jaws. Tails too are all similar – long, straight, often bushy, with a white or black tip. The tail is one of a dog's most important assets and is used for balancing when running fast, for expressing the dog's feelings, and for signaling to other members of the pack. When dogs were domesticated, their appearance changed because certain features were specially selected for each breed. For example, no wild dog has a tail permanently curled over its back.

FUR COATS
Before the present century, for people to keep warm in the winter it was essential to have clothing made from animal furs. Today, with all the artificial materials available, wearing a fur coat shows that the person has no regard for the dwindling numbers of wild animals and little compassion for their suffering.

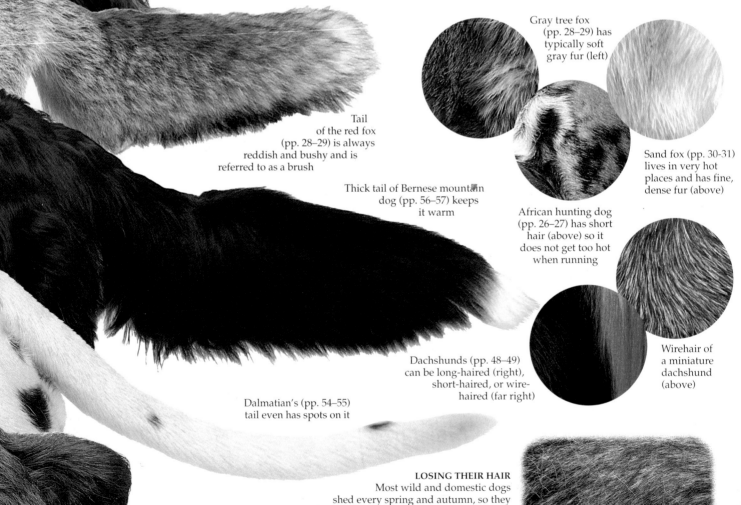

Tails of many domestic dogs – like this Australian terrier (pp. 52–53) – are docked so that the tail stands up straight

Tail of the red fox (pp. 28–29) is always reddish and bushy and is referred to as a brush

Gray tree fox (pp. 28–29) has typically soft gray fur (left)

Sand fox (pp. 30-31) lives in very hot places and has fine, dense fur (above)

Thick tail of Bernese mountain dog (pp. 56–57) keeps it warm

African hunting dog (pp. 26–27) has short hair (above) so it does not get too hot when running

Wirehair of a miniature dachshund (above)

Dachshunds (pp. 48–49) can be long-haired (right), short-haired, or wire-haired (far right)

Dalmatian's (pp. 54–55) tail even has spots on it

LOSING THEIR HAIR
Most wild and domestic dogs shed every spring and autumn, so they have a thin coat in the summer and a thick one in the winter. The fur of this German shepherd (pp. 44–45) is shedding.

Hairy tail of giant schnauzer is cut short by docking (pp. 44–45)

Brain case
(cranium)

Large orbit for eye

Upper jaw

Huge head

Ear bone

Canine tooth

Lower jaw

Side view of skull
of Japanese chin

DOGS' ANCESTOR
Wolves (pp. 22–23)
have typical long
heads and
muzzles.

A JAPANESE CHIN
All dogs are descended
from wolves, even this
Japanese chin, or
spaniel, with its little
round head and short
curved jaws.

Orbit for eye

Upper molar

Canine
tooth

Incisor

Hard palate

Ear bone

Zygomatic arch, or
bony arch at outside
edge of eye socket

Palatal view
(showing roof of
mouth) of skull
of Japanese chin

Powerful
nose

Arctic wolf

DOG SLEUTH
The bloodhound has a
straight head, but not a
pronounced muzzle; it uses
its powerful sense of smell
for tracking (pp. 16–17).

Bloodhound

Palatal view
of bat-eared fox

Small molar for
eating insects

Straight
profile
to head

Incisor

Hard palate

Fox terrier

DIFFERENT TEETH
The bat-eared fox has
teeth that are different from
any other canid (they are smaller,
and there are 4 to 8 more than the
usual 42) but its head is still doglike.

STRAIGHT-LACED
The fox terrier (pp. 52–53)
has been bred to have a
very straight head, with
no angle between the
brain case and the face.

Brain case
(cranium)

Zygomatic arch
of eye socket

Nasal
region

Pekingese

Ear
bone

Flat face

Incisor

Canine
tooth

Side view of skull
of bat-eared fox

Lower jaw

PERKY PEKE
Years of selective
breeding (pp. 58–59)
have given the Pekingese a
small, round head, flat face,
floppy ears, and soft fur.

Sight and sound

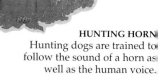

EVERY DOMESTIC DOG IN THE WORLD, whether it is a Pekingese (pp. 58–59) or a Great Dane (pp. 56–57), has inherited the eyes and ears of its wild ancestor, the wolf. All its senses have evolved for being a social hunter of large prey, but these senses have been adapted and developed in different breeds of dog by "artificial selection." This means, for example, that in sight hounds (pp. 48–49), such as greyhounds, puppies with particularly good sight have been chosen over the centuries as future breeders. These breeders then pass on the trait of good sight to their puppies. So in the course of time, greyhounds have developed even better sight than the wolf. Wolves and domestic dogs cannot hear as well as some other carnivores, because they usually hunt at dusk when sight is more important than hearing. Foxes, however, hunt at night, and it is thought that their sense of hearing is more acute than a wolf's.

HUNTING HORN
Hunting dogs are trained to follow the sound of a horn as well as the human voice.

DOG'S WHISTLE
Most dogs will respond to the sound of a whistle.

LISTENING DOG
The large erect ears are turned this way and that as this dog works out where the sounds it is listening to are coming from.

Dense fur keeps the fennec warm on cold nights in the desert

The fennec's light-colored fur is pale to reflect the heat of the desert during the day

FENNEC FOX
The fennec is the smallest member of the fox family. It lives in the Sahara and Arabian deserts and is well adapted for keeping cool and finding any food it can in the hot, dry sand.

The fennec's huge ears allow body heat to escape, which helps to keep the animal cool in the hot desert

Outer ear

Ear muscle

Furry outside of ear

Brain

Bones of the inner ear

Ear canal

Ear cavity of skull

Glands

The belly fur is even paler, to reflect the heat from the ground

THE EAR
All wild members of the dog family have erect ears which help them to tell where a sound has come from.

BEAUTIFUL BORZOI
The borzoi (pp. 46–47) is a typical sight hound, or gazehound. Because of its keen sight it was used in the Middle East for game hunting, and later by Russian royalty in traditional wolf hunts.

The eyes are large and face forward so the borzoi probably has stereoscopic vision, which means that it can see in three dimensions, as humans do

Upper eyelid

Pupil

Iris

Lower eyelid

Third eyelid, or nictitating membrane

THE EYE
Inside a dog's upper and lower eyelids, there is a third eyelid – which protects the eye from dirt and dust.

JACKAL-HEADED GOD OF MUMMIFICATION
Anubis, a jackal-headed god in ancient Egypt, supervised embalming and weighed the hearts of the dead.

Muzzles (pp. 46–47) are usually worn by racing greyhounds

When the upper teeth closely overlap the lower teeth, it is called a scissor bite

A WINNING GREYHOUND
This greyhound is waiting intently for the start of the race, and all its senses are directed forward. As it races it will keep its eyes centered on the mechanical hare as though it were a live animal.

MANED WOLF
The so-called "maned wolf" (pp. 32–33) of the South American savanna has very large ears for hearing the slightest sound in the long grass.

Dog collar

THE CHASE IS ON
This pack of African hunting dogs is chasing a gemsbok. They use their big eyes to see their prey and their large ears to hear the communicating sounds of the pack, and also to hear whether any other predators are trying to take over their prey.

GUARD DOG
This dog – an ancient Roman sculpture – is anxiously watching and listening for any thieves at the door.

On the scent trail

Aʟʟ ᴍᴇᴍʙᴇʀs ᴏꜰ ᴛʜᴇ ᴄᴀɴɪᴅ ᴏʀ ᴅᴏɢ ꜰᴀᴍɪʟʏ have a far better sense of smell than any human, and they probably remember scents better than sights. That is to say, whereas humans remember how objects are placed in a room and what they look like, a dog will remember the arrangement of the objects by their different scents. In all wild canids – wolves, wild dogs, jackals, and foxes – smell is the most highly developed of all the senses. The animal hunts with its nose, finds its mate with its nose, and identifies every new being that comes into its territory with its nose. It can even tell whether other animals are relaxed or afraid by their smell. This intense perception of scent is made possible by the long nose of the skull, which contains rolls of very thin bone over which the particles of scent are drawn. With certain hunting and gun dogs, there has been selection for the sense of smell in preference to the other senses. These dogs, such as the bloodhound, can smell very well but are nearsighted.

WHO ARE YOU?
A dog can learn a lot about another dog by smelling the anal gland just beneath its tail.

Drop ears in scent hounds – such as the beagle – mean that their hearing is not as good as that of a wild dog or fox, with erect ears

Saluki

Dalmatian

TRUFFLE HUNTING
A truffle is a fungus that grows underground and is considered to be a great food delicacy, especially in France, where dogs are trained to search for truffles by their smell.

A nose, close to the ground, picks up the scents of prey

ATTACKING
A fox would not usually attack a sheep, but it might do so if it could smell that the sheep was already dying.

Nasal cavity with paper-thin turbinal bones

Sinuses

Cavity of brain

Fleshy nose

Lip

Palate

NASAL CAVITY
A dog's keen sense of smell is due to rolls of very fine bone, or turbinals, in its nasal cavity. These are connected to a fine mesh of nerve endings attached to the olfactory nerve, which takes scent messages to the brain.

MINI DACHSHUND'S NOSE
Like all of the dog family, this miniature dachshund has a leathery nose and two nostrils through which scents are drawn into the nasal cavity.

The bat-eared fox's keen sense of smell allows it to find its prey quickly

BAT-EARED FOX
The bat-eared fox eats any small animal or fruit that it can find, and it needs a keen sense of smell to look for beetles underground.

Strong legs and excellent stamina make the beagle a dependable hunter

BEAGLE
Scent hounds, like this beagle, have been bred to use their noses more than their eyes and ears in the hunt. Because of this well-developed sense of smell, they can pursue small game very successfully. And with less keen hearing, the dog can concentrate on tracking a scent without being distracted by slight noises.

Looking for prey . . .

. . . and finding a surprise

ENGLISH SETTER
Like the pointer, the setters are scent hounds. They are trained to "set up" game birds from the ground so they can be shot in the air.

Behavior

THE DOG FAMILY can be divided into two distinct groups according to behavior: solitary hunters and social hunters. The solitary hunters – that is, the foxes and South American wild dogs (pp. 28–33) – live on their own, except when they are mating and rearing their young. The wolf, jackal, coyote, African hunting dog, dhole (pp. 22–27), and the domestic dog (pp. 14–17) are all social hunters. Their behavior is in many ways like that of a human family in which the parents are the leaders and the children do as they are told until they are old enough to leave and form their own family groups. In a wolf pack, or a family of African hunting dogs, every individual knows which other dog is above or below it in the family hierarchy, and it will fight hard to keep or to better its position. Even though wolves are such powerful killers, fights between them seldom end in death, and if one wolf is injured the others will often help it to feed.

Ears back show dog is afraid – or even potentially aggressive

Dog appears happy and relaxed – with pert ears and smiling mouth

Crossbred dog

GETTING TO KNOW YOU
The strong, dominant wolf on the left is greeting the weaker, more submissive wolf on the right.

Ears laid back show fear or aggression

Tail between legs shows dog in a submissive stance

Mouth shut tightly denotes apprehension

German shepherd

BODY LANGUAGE
Even though dogs cannot speak like humans, they say all they need to each other by the postures of their bodies and tails.

JUST GOOD FRIENDS
This charming painting by English artist John Charlton (1849–1917) shows three dogs of indistinct breeds (pp. 60–61) playing together in the snow and exhibiting their friendly relationship with one another.

Crouched body means fox is waiting to pounce

Alert ears show fox is listening for potential prey

Solitary hunters

Foxes, including this American gray fox (pp. 28–29), are solitary hunters that kill their prey by themselves. They do not, therefore, have the complicated interactive behavior of the social hunters. A fox's tail cannot wag as expressively as a wolf's, and its upright ears are not as mobile. Even so, if a fox is frightened it will cower down to make itself look small, and if it is angry it will stand up as tall as it can to look large and threatening.

Gray tree-climbing fox

Social hunters

The African hunting dog and other social hunters not only have to provide enough meat for the family group but they must also compete for food with, and defend themselves against, other large predators, like lions and hyenas. Human hunters have always been the main competitors of social hunters. The wolf (pp. 22–23) has been exterminated over much of its vast range in Europe and Asia, and the African hunting dog and the dhole (pp. 26–27) are also near extinction. Only jackals and the coyote (pp. 24–25), being smaller and more adaptable, continue to flourish.

Two wolves fighting it out to see which one will be the leader

HOWLIN' WOLVES
Like its wolf ancestors, this pointer will howl if left on its own in an effort to communicate with others of its kind. Some dogs will also howl when they hear certain kinds of music or, if they are kept outside, when the moon is full.

TOP DOG
Although much smaller than the Dalmatian, this Norfolk terrier has the stronger personality and is showing that he is top dog.

Dalmatian's head is slightly turned away, showing fear

Norfolk terrier's positive stance shows his confidence toward the larger dog

Dalmatian

Norfolk terrier

FIGHTING FOR A BITE
At a kill, these African hunting dogs will eat vast quantities of meat, which is later regurgitated, or vomited up, for their young, or for other members of the pack, who will fight over the half-digested morsels.

Pointer

DOGS' SOCIAL CLUB
This caricature by J. J. Granville, published in Paris, France, in 1859, emphasizes the similarity of dog behavior with that of humans.

Cubs and puppies

THE PUPPIES AND CUBS of all members of the dog family (Canidae) look similar when they are new-born. They are small, defenseless, and blind, and have short hair, short legs, and a little tail. At first, like all mammals, the cubs or puppies, which may vary in number from one to twelve or more, can only suck milk from their mother's nipples. After a few days (about nine for a domestic dog) their eyes open, they begin to hear, and they soon need more solid food. This is provided by the mother, and in social species by other members of the group, who re-gurgitate (vomit up) meat that they have previously eaten. A mother dog who looks as though she is being sick in front of her puppies is not ill but rather is providing them with their first solid meal. In the wild the young are nearly always born in a den or hole in the ground, and in the same way, a domestic dog needs a dark, warm place where she can give birth, which will happen about 63 days after she has been mated.

Four-week-old Great Dane puppies . . .

. . . playfully attacking each other . . .

IT'S PLAYTIME
It is essential that all puppies be allowed space in which to play. They must have exercise in order to grow properly, but of equal importance is their need to learn social interaction with other dogs and with humans. In this playing sequence, two Great Dane puppies (four weeks old) are learning to relate to each other.

. . . with one trying to dominate the other

LOOKING ENDEARING
The puppies of a Great Dane (above and right) are no dif-ferent in their needs from a Pekingese or a wolf. But, as they are the giants among dogs, they require a great deal of wholesome meat, extra calcium and vitamins, and large bones to chew (pp. 62–63). They also need plenty of space in which to play and exercise their growing limbs.

All is well – they're friends again

Six-week-old
Great Dane puppies

NURSING MOTHER
This mother wolf is contentedly suckling her cubs, but in a few weeks their sharp little milk teeth will have grown and will hurt her nipples. Then she will begin to wean the cubs with regurgitated meat.

LEARNING TO BEHAVE
The play of these African hunting dog pups is a school for adult life in which they must be powerful hunters. Just as with the Great Dane puppies, they learn the rules of social behavior from their games.

A small bronze Greek sculpture of a pregnant female – from the fifth century B.C.

Four-and-a-half-month-old black Labrador puppy

Dalmatian at six months

GETTING CARRIED AWAY
All members of the dog family will carry their cubs around. Usually, it is the mother, but sometimes the father will also take the cub gently by the scruff of its neck with his teeth and carry it to safety.

WOLF-BOYS
Legend has it that the city of Rome in Italy was founded in 753 B.C. by two brothers – Romulus and Remus – who had been suckled as babies by a she-wolf.

A TAIL OF TWO PUPPIES
These puppies are play fighting. The Dalmatian is a little older than the black Labrador retriever and is the dominant dog. Both of them are about half-grown, and in a few months they could be fighting in earnest.

Leader of the pack

FOLLOW THE LEADER
This group of European wolves is following the leader on the way to look for prey in the forest. They will eat anything they can find – from an elk to a mouse – and if food is really scarce they will even eat insects and berries. Wolves will range over a huge area, up to 400 sq miles (1,000 sq km), in packs that can be as large as 20 individuals.

THE WOLF PACK is similar to a human family group, in which the oldest male and the oldest female are the leaders, and the young must do as they are told. Wolves and humans have many patterns of social behavior in common, for both evolved as social hunters who had to work together in a team so they could kill animals larger than themselves. Wolves guard their territory closely and make their presence known by howling (pp. 18–19). Each member of the pack knows his or her position in the scale of dominance, and any wolf that tries to assert itself is likely to be expelled from the pack by the leaders. The only pair of wolves to mate are the dominant male and the dominant female, and after the cubs are born the father will bring meat back to the den for the mother. The cubs are suckled for about 10 weeks; the mother and the younger wolves will feed them with regurgitated meat (partly digested meat returned to the mouth from the stomach) until they are old enough to hunt with the pack. At first, the young cubs can behave as they like and all the wolves will put up with their play fights, but as they grow older they too must learn to keep their place.

Ears are erect to show that the wolf is on the alert – either for prey or foe

EUROPEAN GRAY WOLF
In earlier times there were wolves in every country in Europe, but these wonderfully intelligent animals have been slaughtered by farmers and hunters for hundreds of years and they are now found only in limited quantities in southern and eastern Europe.

Sharp teeth enable wolf to kill its prey quickly

A WOLF OF MANY COLORS
The Arctic wolf from the far north of Canada has a hard life trying to find prey in the freezing cold of the Arctic. These wolves have a very thick white winter coat to camouflage them in the snow and ice, although during the summer they can be shades of gray or buff, or occasionally even black. They have short tails and small ears to keep the body as compact as possible. Arctic wolves feed on hares and birds, and sometimes, if they are lucky, a pack will be able to kill a deer or a musk ox.

LITTLE RED RIDING HOOD
When there really were wolves in the forests, mothers would have told their children the story of Little Red Riding Hood – of how she was tricked by a very clever wolf – to frighten them from going out alone.

WINNER OR LOSER
Wolves are quick to snarl at each other, and they fight fairly often. But although a wolf can be seriously hurt in a fight, seldom will it be killed.

A RARE RED WOLF
The red wolf is smaller than the gray wolf and is adapted for living in the warmer climate of the southeastern U.S. It was extinct in the wild, but in 1988 a few were reintroduced into North Carolina.

TROUBLE AHEAD FOR BRAVE NOVICE
According to the legends of the Nootka Indians of the Northwest, novices were sometimes carried away by wolves. This club may have been used as a display object to represent the powers the brave received during his captivity. It is made of abalone shell, bone, and human hair, and a wolf's head is carved at one end.

TERROR OF WEREWOLVES
According to folklore, a werewolf is a person who has changed into a wolf, or is capable of taking the shape of a wolf, while keeping its human intelligence. Many horror films have been made about werewolves.

The legs have to be long and very powerful so the wolf can range over huge distances in search of prey

MAKING A MEAL OF IT
A pack of wolves chase musk oxen on Ellesmere Island in the Arctic in the hope of finding food.

The tail of this wolf is pointing down, showing it is wary of what is ahead

Jackals and coyotes

Limestone stele of Egyptian kneeling before the jackal of Wepwawet, with 63 other jackals, made after 550 B.C.

JACKALS, AND THE COYOTE, which lives only in North America, come below the wolf in the scale of social hunters (pp. 18–19) – the wolf being the most social of all animals that hunt on land. There are four species of jackals, all of which are found in Africa. The most widespread is the golden jackal, which is found in southeastern Europe and southern Asia as well as in Africa. Both the side-striped jackal and the black-backed jackal are found in Africa, south of the Sahara. The fourth jackal, the Simien jackal, lives only on the high plains of the Simen Mountains in Ethiopia, in the eastern part of Africa, and it is now in danger of extinction (pp. 12–13). All species of jackals, and the coyote, live in close-knit family groups which forage for any food they can find. Meals may vary from the carcass of an animal long since dead and left unwanted by other carnivores, to an antelope that the canids themselves have managed to kill. When a litter of pups is born (pp. 20–21), all the jackals in the family will help to look after them and bring back food for them to the den.

GOLDEN OLDIES
This pair of golden jackals will stay together for their whole lives, hunting and breeding together, unless one of them is killed. They will patrol their territory together, scent mark it with their urine, and prevent any intruding jackals from coming near.

SILVER SADDLE
The black-backed jackal has a spectacular coat of fine fur with a silver and black saddle. It lives on open grasslands in eastern and southern Africa.

This mummified canid in the form of the jackal god, Anubis, is from ancient Egypt (pp. 14-15), between 600 B.C. and A.D. 300

SOCIAL COYOTE

The name "coyote" comes from the Aztec word, *coyotl*. The coyote – also called a brush, or prairie, wolf – is the jackal of North America and, like the jackal, it is a social hunter (pp. 18–19) that lives in pairs and family groups.

CUNNING COYDOG

Wild coyotes sometimes mate with domestic dogs and produce "coydog" pups. As they are neither wild nor tame, coydogs have a hard time and often take to killing domestic livestock for food.

Skull is smaller than a wolf's and has a flat forehead and comparatively small teeth

CANID QUICKSTEP

This golden jackal is doing a quick turn in its lookout for prey.

DOG DANCE

Dogs were highly regarded by native North Americans, both for their meat and for transportation (pp. 56–57). This painting by the Swiss artist Karl Bodmer (1809–1893) shows a medicine man of the Hidatsa tribe wearing a special costume and performing a "dog dance." The Hidatsa tribe lived along the Missouri River in North Dakota.

Golden jackal's coarse, short-haired coat varies in color from pale golden brown to brown-tipped yellow, depending on season and region

ETHIOPIAN HOWLER

The Simien jackal is in danger of extinction (pp. 12–13) because more and more of the high grassland plains where it lives are being taken over by farmers for livestock grazing. There may be only about 500 of these distinctive, tawny-red coated jackals left in the wild.

JACKAL WORSHIP

Anubis, the jackal god, is frequently shown in ancient Egyptian artifacts.

African and Asian dogs

THERE ARE MANY WILD CANIDS, aside from jackals (pp. 24–25) and wolves (pp. 22–23), living in Africa and Asia. In Africa there is the hunting dog (pp. 6–7) and the bat-eared fox (pp. 14–17) – which is not really a fox and has teeth that are different from those of all other wild dogs. In India and Southeast Asia there is the dhole, or red dog, as well as the raccoon dog, which comes from eastern Asia and Japan. All these wild dogs are social hunters. The Tibetan fox, from the high mountains of Tibet, and the Bengal fox are true foxes (pp. 28–29) and are solitary hunters (pp. 18–19) of small animals. Each of the many species of wild dog that lives in Asia and Africa is a carnivore with a specialized way of life that has evolved, or changed over many years. Each fills an ecological niche, or well-defined place, among the plants and other animals in its environment. Each wild dog or fox hunts its prey but is also hunted by other predators in its surroundings. In this way the population of any one group of animals does not grow too large, and the balance of nature is maintained.

SOUTHERN SOLITAIRE
The Cape fox of South Africa is the most southern of the true foxes. It is a small solitary hunter (pp. 18–19) with a silvery coat. The Cape fox lives in dry places and hunts at dusk.

Large, rounded ears

Short, broad face and muzzle

Thin but well-muscled legs

Unique coat pattern is tan and gray with large white blotches

Having only four toes on the front foot makes the hunting dog unique among the dog family

White tuft at the end of the short bushy tail acts as a flag

African hunting dog

A MOST SOCIABLE DOG
The African hunting dog is one of the most social of all members of the dog family. However, it is not a true dog, or canid (because it did not descend from the wolf); it belongs in a group of its own, the genus *Lycaon*. These dogs live in large family packs on grasslands and have an elaborate system of communication by means of body movements and sounds. Hunting by day, they range over a huge area in search of prey. They are vulnerable to disease and parasites, to other hungry carnivores (such as lions), and to human hunters.

Bat-eared fox

Very large ears, up to 5 in (12 cm) long

Dark gray to black on face mask and muzzle

Very long tail – up to 13 in (34 cm) in length

ENOUGH TEETH
The bat-eared fox (pp. 16–17) has 46 to 50 teeth – compared to 42 in other species of canid. It feeds mostly on insects but will also eat fruits.

TWO-HEADED FETISH
This *Konde*, or dog-shaped medicine figure, from Bakongo in Zaire, Africa, is used by driving nails into its wooden body to activate the magical healing forces within.

INDIAN OR CHINESE?
The dhole, or red dog, is a social hunter (pp. 18–19) with some characteristics like the African hunting dog, although apart from the rounded ears, they do not look at all alike. Neither of these canids will interbreed with domestic dogs. The Chinese dhole has a thicker, darker coat than the more southern Indian dhole.

Rounded ears

Dark red coat

Long, bushy tail

Chinese dhole

Tawny-colored coat

Indian dhole

Tail is darker color than rest of coat

ON TOP OF THE WORLD
The Tibetan fox lives on the high, icy-cold plateaus of Tibet above 12,000 ft (4,000 m). It has a very thick, furry coat to keep it warm and long, slender jaws for pulling small rodents out of their burrows.

Tail is short, relative to its body length

White variety of coat shows this dog has been bred in captivity for its fur

Short, sharply pointed muzzle

Raccoon dog in winter coat

WHEN IS A RACCOON NOT A RACCOON?
The raccoon dog (above and right) has this name because it looks similar to a raccoon. It is a chubby canid with a short tail and a very thick, fine coat of gray-black and white fur. Because the coat is highly valued by fur traders (pp. 12–13), the raccoon dog has been bred in captivity in many countries. In the U.S.S.R., captive animals were allowed to go free and are now living as wild populations (pp. 36–37) which are spreading westward.

Short, erect ears rounded at top

ONE LITTLE INDIAN
The Bengal fox is like a small red fox. It lives on open grasslands and scrub in India and digs its own dens. Like all foxes it hunts rodents, lizards, and other small animals.

Black facial mask, like that of a true raccoon

True raccoon of North and South America belongs to the Procyonidae family

Raccoon dog in dark summer coat

27

Red fox, gray fox

ALL FOXES ARE SOLITARY HUNTERS that live on their own (pp. 18–19) – except in the mating season. They have long bodies, sharply pointed faces, and a bushy tail which is often called a "brush." Foxes have highly developed senses (pp. 14–17) and large, erect ears. Their usual prey are rodents and rabbits. The red fox is one of the most common carnivores in the world and is known to most people from fables and stories for its cunning. Besides the red fox there are nine other species in the fox group – or the genus *Vulpes* (pp. 26–27, 30–31). The gray fox of North and Central America belongs to another group – the genus *Urocyon*. It has different habits from the red fox and is noted for its ability to climb trees. The red fox is very adaptable and can live in many different environments from deserts and mountains to the centers of cities.

THE QUACK FROG
This is one of Greek storyteller Aesop's (620–560 B.C.) many fables. It tells the story of a frog who claimed to be a learned doctor. The fox asked him why, if he was so skilled, did he not heal his own strange walk and wrinkled skin.

WAITING FOR LUNCH
Fox cubs (pp. 20–21) will stay with their mother for several months before they must leave her and find their own territories.

MAKING TRACKS
The paw prints of a fox are smaller than those of most dogs – the marks of the pads are longer, and the claws are sharply pointed.

Coat can range in color from grayish and rust-red to a flame red

FURRY BEAUTIFUL
The red fox's fur is so beautiful that for thousands of years people have made clothes for themselves from their pelts. Captive foxes have also been bred for their furs in a variety of different coat colors. Nowadays, clothes made of animal furs are unacceptable to many people who care about animals (pp. 12–13).

The tail of the red fox, which always has a white tip, does not express the animal's feelings the way the tail of a dog does

GETTING TO THE TOP
The gray tree fox is found in the United States (except in the Rocky Mountains and the Northwest), Central America, and northern South America. It is a little smaller than the red fox and has a salt-and-pepper coat with a reddish belly.

A gray tree-climbing fox on the lookout for prey, which can be rabbits, insects, or carrion (dead animals)

Tip of the tail may be black, or grayish like the coat, but it is never white

Nose and sides of muzzle are black

A BIRD IN VIEW
The red fox (left) does not climb trees (whereas the gray fox spends much of its time in trees looking for birds and eggs to eat) – from a scene printed on an English Wedgwood plate, c.1764.

Fox's acute sense of smell (pp. 16–17) encourages it to cover distances of up to 6 miles (10 km) in search of food

Throat and chin have white or light-colored fur

A-HUNTING WE SHALL GO
In many countries fox hunting (pp. 14–15) is part of the sporting life of the country-side. Because they are such successful carnivores, foxes can become a pest to farmers by killing chickens and game birds. Hunting controls the numbers of foxes, but many people think it is cruel.

STREET-WISE
In some cities foxes are becoming increasingly common. They kill rats, scavenge for food from garbage cans, and even seem to learn road sense.

BLACK OR RED?
American artist John James Audubon (1785–1851) painted a wide variety of wildlife, including the black, or melanistic, form of the red fox.

DEEP IN THE FOREST
English artist William Morris (1834–1896), who designed this tapestry, had a great regard for the natural world. To him, as to many people today, the fox was an essential part of every woodland scene.

Hot foxes, cold foxes

NOT ALL SPECIES OF FOXES live in the temperate (moderate) parts of the world and feed off the abundant rats, mice, and small birds there. A few foxes live exceedingly harsh lives in the coldest – as well as in the hottest – lands. Only one fox lives in the icy cold Arctic regions of Alaska, Canada, northern Europe, and Asia, and that is the Arctic fox. Arctic foxes have been known to cover a territory of 15,000 acres (6,000 hectares) in their search for food; they have small ears, which cut down on heat loss, and dense fur, which keeps them warm in winter. There are also a number of different species of fox that live in the world's hottest deserts. Generally, very little food is available for these foxes, so they have evolved as hunters and scavengers; they range over huge areas in search of some food to keep them alive. Foxes that live in hot, dry deserts all have very large ears which help keep them cool, small bodies that can survive on little food, and short, dense fur. They sleep in dens, or hollows in the sand, during the intense heat of the day, and hunt by night when it can actually be very cold.

DESERT FOX
The fennec fox is the smallest of all the foxes, and it probably has the most difficult time of all in finding food. It lives in the parched Arabian and Sahara deserts where there are very few other animals, so food is always scarce

Soft, dense coat is designed to keep the Arctic fox warm and is thicker in winter

Short, furry ears cut down heat loss – in winter they must not become frost-bitten

Dark brown and white summer coat

Arctic fox cub in dark summer coat

Adult's tail is very bushy, and can be as long as 12 in (30 cm)

COAT OF MANY COLORS *above and right*
The Arctic fox can be seen here in four different colored coats. The fox on the right has the polar, or white, form of its winter coat and lives in the high Arctic where there is nearly always snow on the ground. In the summer, this fox will have a brown and white coat, as above. There is another less common variety of Arctic fox which is called "blue." The winter coat of the "blue" fox is steely gray, but in summer it is all brown. Shedding occurs twice a year – in spring and autumn – when it is time for a color change.

A pair of Arctic foxes – one in a dark summer coat, the other in a pale winter coat

Hind foot has a thick covering of soft fur all over it – even under the pads

Big ears of the sand fox are typical of "hot foxes" – but they're not as big as those of the fennec

HALF A FENNEC FOX, HALF A RED FOX
Often confused with the fennec, this small desert fox from North Africa and the Arabian Desert actually shares many characteristics with the red fox (pp. 28–29). Although its skull, teeth, and coloring are similar to the red fox's, this sand fox has a smaller body, is more delicately built, and has much bigger ears.

A WHITER SHADE OF PALE
The pale fox lives in grasslands at the southern edge of the Sahara Desert in Africa. Like the fennec, it is a small, pale-colored fox.

Long bushy tail can be curled around the body to keep it warm during cold desert nights

Rüppell's sand fox

Thick ruff of very fine fur around the neck

AFTER A MEAL
The fennec must have sharp senses (pp. 14–15) and quick movements if it is to catch these jumping rodents.

SWIFTLY, SWIFTLY
The kit, or swift, fox is the only desert fox in North America. Today, it is found only in the southwestern U.S. and Mexico. It used to be much more widespread until poisoned bait, meant for wolves and coyotes, also killed many kit foxes.

The kit fox lives in the deserts of North America

Adult Arctic fox in pale winter coat

Thick fur on feet almost hides claws

South American mix

SOUTH AMERICAN WILD DOGS are often referred to as foxes or zorros (the Spanish name for foxes), but they should not be confused with either true wolves (pp. 22–23) or true foxes (pp. 28–29). They are solitary hunters (pp. 18–19) of small animals, but they will also eat anything edible that they can find, including fruit. There are four distinct genera, or groups, of foxlike dogs: the short-legged bush dog; the maned wolf; at least six different members of the *Dusicyon* genus, of which the most common is the culpeo; and the doglike, crab-eating (or forest) zorro, which is in the *Cerdocyon* genus. This crab-eating zorro is sometimes tamed by the Indians and will go hunting with them like a domestic dog. Another zorro that used to live on South America's Falkland Islands until the late 1800s was exterminated by fur traders. Charles Darwin (1809–1882), English naturalist and author of *The Origin of Species*, visited the Falklands in 1834 on his voyage around the world in the ship HMS *Beagle*, and described this animal as the "Falkland Island wolf."

CULPEO'S COAT
The culpeo's grayish yellow and black coat, with a black-tipped tail, is not in demand for making fur clothing (pp. 12–13), so this canid is not, at present, in danger of extermination.

Stirrup cup – with a fox on man's forehead – from Mochica tribe of pre-Columbian Peru, A.D. 300–1000

PRETTY PATAGONIAN
The Patagonian fox, or chilla, lives in the southern part of South America. Like many canids in the genus *Dusicyon*, it is not at all timid. In 1834, Darwin killed one by walking close and hitting it on the head with a hammer.

HEAVILY HUNTED
Found in the pampas of Argentina and southern Brazil, this gray-bodied, red-headed fox, or zorro, has a very long, bushy tail.

Azara's zorro

Small ears

Broad face

Bush dog

Reddish tan, or tawny, coat

Very short legs

BUSH BADGER
The bush dog looks more like an otter or badger than a dog. Like other South American members of the dog family, this animal is not a true dog or fox, but belongs in a group – the genus *Speothos* – on its own. It is found in open country near water in tropical South America and spends much of its time in a burrow.

Large, erect ears with white fur inside

Erect mane with darker fur running down nape of neck and back

Dark muzzle

A DOG OF LITTLE EARS
The small-eared dog, or zorro, is one of the rarest of the South American dog family. It lives in the tropical rain forests, but nothing is known of its habits.

MAGNIFICENT MANE
The maned wolf – in the genus *Chrysocyon* – is different from all other members of the dog family in that its tail is very short and its legs are longer than the length of its body. This animal is not a wolf and it is not a fox, though it is sometimes called the "stilt-legged fox." The maned wolf lives in the tall grass and woodlands of southern Brazil and hunts by pouncing on small animals.

Maned wolf

Very long, stilt-like legs

Reddish yellow coat

Maned wolf's short, bushy tail has mostly white fur at its tip

Nazca pottery fox from coast of Peru, 500 B.C. – A.D. 600

Dark-colored fur on legs and feet make it look as if it is wearing stockings

THE CRAB-EATING ZORRO
This brindled gray, crab-eating fox probably does not often eat crabs, so forest fox is a better name. It is a doglike creature and lives in the tropical forests of northeastern South America.

Early domestication

Egyptian papyrus, c.1500–1200 B.C.,
showing two jackals and some goats

THE WOLF IS THE ANCESTOR of all domestic dogs (pp. 48–61), including the Irish wolfhound, which is much larger than the wolf, and the Pekingese, which is very much smaller. The outward appearance of these breeds may look completely different from the wolf and from each other, but every dog, inside its skin, feels and behaves like a wolf. Humans probably first began to live closely with tamed wolves during the last Ice Age, more than 12,000 years ago, and the bones of these early dogs are sometimes found on archeological sites. The people of ancient Egypt and western Asia were the first to begin breeding distinctive kinds of dogs such as mastiffs and greyhounds. Most of the different shapes and sizes of dogs known today were already in existence by the first century B.C. This is known from the skeletal remains of these dogs, but more especially from models, paintings, and other works of art which often portray the animals in marvelous detail. In the ancient world, dogs were kept for hunting, herding, protection (pp. 40–45), sport (pp. 46–47), and, as today, companionship.

JACKAL GO
The jackal ha always had a clos association wit humans, though is not an ancestor o the domestic dog Anubis, the jackal god was a most importan ancient Egyptian deit (god). This one is mad of limestone, A.D. 300

Handle decorated with coral

PERSIAN PLAQUE
This stylized half-dog, half-bird – or "fenmurv" – is a fertility symbol. It is made of silver, c.7th century A.D., sometime during the Sassanid dynasty, and was found in northern India.

FRENCH FLAGON
This Celtic drinking vessel, made of bronze, c.400 B.C., was found near Basse-Yutz in France. Along the handle, two hounds chase a duck which seems to be swimming when liquid is poured.

ANCIENT HUNTSMEN
Assyrian huntsmen walk with their mastiff-like hounds in a royal park in this bas-relief from a palace at Nineveh, the ancient capital of Assyria, built between 645–635 B.C.

EASTERN WORSHIP

In the Far East, dogs are used for many purposes and the images of dogs are included in religious worship. This stone temple god, in the form of a lionlike dog, is from Thailand.

GREEK URN

This beautiful vase is of Greek design (c.380–360 B.C.), though it was found in southern Italy. The young girl is dangling a tortoise to tease her pet dog. The bracelets on her ankle are to ward off evil spirits.

The Townley hounds sculpture, collected by the Englishman Charles Townley (1737–1805), was found at Monte Cagnolo near Rome, Italy, during the late 1700s

ONE WOMAN AND HER DOG

This is the skeleton of a woman who was buried with her hand resting on the body of her dog. The skeletons were found in Israel on an archeological site called Ein Mallaha and date back to about 12,000 years ago. This is one of the earliest examples of a domestic dog ever to be discovered in the world.

TOWNLEY HOUNDS

The Romans kept dogs from the earliest times. They used greyhounds and bloodhounds for hunting; large mastiffs were thought of as ideal not only as fighting dogs but also in war. This exquisite marble sculpture from Rome, 2nd century A.D., is of a pair of seated greyhounds.

Italian brass collar

German spiked iron collar

DOGS' COLLARS

Dogs have been wearing collars ever since Egyptian times. We know this because dogs in art have been depicted wearing collars – from a painting found in Pompeii to relatively modern paintings and sculptures.

DOG ROSE

The ancient Greeks thought this flower had magical qualities and used it to treat people who had been bitten by a rabid dog (pp. 62–63).

CAVE CANEM

Just as today "Beware of the dog" is written on gates, the Romans wrote *Cave canem*, which means the same in Latin. This mosaic, c.4th century A.D., comes from an entrance hall of a villa, excavated in Bodrum in Turkey.

Silver presentation collar

Pottery vessel – from the Colima culture in Mexico, A.D. 300–900 – of a hairless "techichi" dog

Feral dogs

AFTER THE FIRST DOGS were domesticated about 12,000 years ago, some of them, like the dingo, eventually reverted to life in the wild. They are known as "feral" dogs. They hunted for their own food except when they could scavenge for a few scraps left by human hunters. In many parts of the world, dogs still live like this. Many populations of dogs live and breed without any human contact at all. The most successful of all feral dogs is the dingo of Australia, but there are also feral dogs in India and many other parts of Asia, where they are called "pariah" dogs – "pariah" is a Tamil, or Sri Lankan, word meaning "outcast." All over Africa feral dogs live on the outskirts of villages, where they serve a useful function in cleaning up all the garbage. At times these dogs are allowed into the houses, but they are seldom given anything to eat because there is often not enough food for the people, let alone the animals. So the dogs must fend for themselves.

FERRETING FOR FOOD
The feral dogs of Egypt are sometimes lucky and find scraps of food left by tourists.

IN THE WILDS OF INDIA
Pariah dogs have been living wild in India for thousands of years. Some look like the dingoes of Australia.

SANTO DOMINGO DOG
This dog must have looked very similar to the wild dogs that Christopher Columbus (1451–1506) probably found in the West Indies when he discovered America.

PERUVIAN PARIAH
Long before the Spanish first went to South America, the native peoples had dogs that lived around the settlements, just as their descendants, the feral dogs of today, do.

QUINKAN SPIRITS
In these cave paintings near Cape York in Australia, these "Quinkan spirits" – the Great Ancestors of the aborigines – are accompanied by a dingo.

Nose is used for sniffing prey, such as lizards, rabbits, or rodents, or even fruit and plants

A sitting dingo

Eye of a dingo is more like that of a wolf than a dog

DOMINANT DINGO
These young dingoes know which one is the dominant dog.

THE AUSTRALIAN DOG

The dingoes of Australia (above and right) have been so successful at living in the wild that it has only recently been recognized that they were originally domestic dogs taken to Australia by the native aborigines at least 4,000 years ago. Dingoes should be preserved as part of the unique animal kingdom of Australia because – except where they have interbred with European dogs – they are probably the only remaining purebred descendants of prehistoric domestic dogs.

THE ARISTOCRAT OF DOGS
The dingo, as depicted in this old engraving, is the aristocrat of all breeds. It is the most purebred dog in the world, because there are no other wild dogs with which it can breed.

MOTHER AND BABIES
Like all dogs, the dingo is descended from the wolf (pp. 22–23). Like the wolf, the dingo mates once a year and brings up its young to be social hunters (pp. 18–19).

Coat is a tawny yellow with pale underparts

Dingo's feet are like a wolf's – there is no dewclaw (pp. 6–7) on the hind foot

Tail is long and bushy – sometimes with a white tip

Feet are white

Development of breeds

Elegant lurcher shows typical bone structure of a dog

Many breeds of dogs are hundreds of years old, such as spaniels, greyhounds, and terriers, but a new breed can be developed at any time by crossing two or more different breeds. The Sealyham terrier is one example of a new breed of terrier (pp. 52–53) that was developed in the 1800s in Sealyham, Wales. It is also possible to reconstitute, or "remake," a breed that has become extinct. For example, the Irish wolfhound, which died out about a hundred years ago, was reconstituted as a new line from a cross of Great Danes, deerhounds, and mastiffs (pp. 48–49). Prior to the first dog show in England in 1859, there was considerable variation in the size, shape, and color of dogs within a single breed. Today, however, the dogs within one breed all look very similar because of the required standards for showing. Standardizing can be harmful to breeds, as the dogs lose their individual characteristics. It can also lead to inherited ailments and is why German shepherds are prone to dislocated hips.

The turned-up corners of the mouth make this lurcher look as if it is smiling

IT'S RAINING CATS, DOGS, AND PITCHFORKS
This old English saying may be based on the ancient Chinese spirits for rain and wind, which were sometimes depicted as a cat and a dog. Here, the English caricaturist George Cruikshank (1792–1878) offers his interpretation.

Lurcher

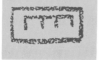

SECRET SYMBOLS
American "kings of the road" – tramps, or hobos – used secret signs to let their friends know whether there was a dog (left), or a bad dog (below), on a stranger's property.

Dog

Bad dog

Wedgwood majolica (highly glazed earthenware) punch bowl, decorated with puppet Punch and his clown-dog Toby

BULL'S-EYE
This bull terrier starred with Oliver Reed, who played Sikes in the 1968 film *Oliver!*, based on a novel by English writer Charles Dickens (1812–1870). Bull terriers were developed in the 1700s by crossing bulldogs and terrier types to produce a fierce fighting dog (pp. 46–47). Their small, fine, erect ears were developed to avoid illegal ear-cropping (pp. 44–45).

A FIGHT TO THE FINISH
The Staffordshire bull terrier first entered the show ring as a recognized breed in 1935. It was developed in the Midlands of England, originally as a fighting dog, by crossing the old-fashioned bull terrier with the bulldog and the now-extinct Old English terrier.

Very muscular body

Small, half-pricked ears

Staffordshire bull terrier

Dark, deep-set eyes

V-shaped ears, falling forward

THE ROUGH AND THE SMOOTH
These popular terriers were first bred in the 1800s by Jack Russell, a clergyman from Devon, England. These small dogs were a cross between several now-extinct breeds and varied much in appearance and size. Kennel clubs are beginning to recognize the Jack Russell as an official breed – for example, the British Kennel Club made the Parson Jack Russell (but not all Jack Russells) an official breed in 1990, but in the U.S. and Canada the Jack Russell is still not recognized as an official breed for showing.

Coat can be long and rough-haired, or short and smooth-haired

Jack Russell terriers

Streamlined body and short-haired coat make a dog built for speed

Thomas Bewick's (pp. 42–43) engraving of an old-fashioned lurcher

IN THE LURCH
The lurcher was originally a crossbreed (pp. 60–61) between a greyhound and a terrier; its patience, intelligence, speed, and fighting ability made it a perfect dog for a poacher (pp. 40–41). Many owners would like to enter their lurchers in the show ring, but as yet they are still not recognized as an official breed.

HEAD OVER HEELS
It's hard to say what breed this little dog is – but he has certainly surprised his mistress with his amusing antics.

Hunting dogs

HUNTING IN INDIA
The Mogul emperors of India had just as many rituals of hunting as the feudal lords of medieval Europe. Akbar (1542–1605) is shown here hunting black buck, or Indian antelope, with Saluki-type hounds.

MEDIEVAL HUNTING DOGS
Medieval hunters usually had a pack of at least 12 running hounds and a well-trained scent hound, or lyam-hound, whose task was to frighten the game out of its hiding place. In this detail of a picture in *Benninck's Book of Hours*, the game is a wild boar.

F OR CENTURIES DOGS were used for hunting wild animals all over the world. In medieval times, hunting from horseback with dogs became an important part of life for the kings and feudal lords of Europe. Hunting was considered necessary as training for tournaments of chivalry and for warfare. The laws of hunting, or venery as it was called then, were very complicated; certain animals were preserved for only the nobility to hunt. Important "beasts of venery" were the red deer stag (male) and hind (female), the hare, wild boar, and wolf. The fallow deer, roe deer, fox, and wildcat were considered of secondary value and were called "beasts of the chase." Special breeds of scent and sight hounds (pp. 14–17) were used at different times during these hunts and were kept in royal kennels. The most valuable dogs were those trained to hunt large game.

COME BLOW THE HORN
Blowing the horn with a series of long and short notes was a very important part of the rituals of medieval hunting.

The Savernake Horn was made of ivory in 12th-century England. Hunting scenes engraved in silver were added in the 14th century

THE THRILL OF THE CHASE
A horse, rider, and hunting dogs chase a stag along this French watch chain, beautifully crafted in silver and gold in 1845.

GAMEKEEPER AND HIS DOGS
Many traditions connected with hunting and shooting remain unchanged since medieval times. The gamekeeper's job of protecting game from predators and poachers is still the same as it was when the laws of venery were first enacted in the 11th century.

BENIN PIECE
The Benin bronzes from Nigeria are famous throughout the world for their great artistic value. This bronze plaque, made by a Nigerian artist in the late 16th century, is of a Portuguese soldier with his gun and hunting dog.

RUNNING WITH THE PACK
This late 19th-century painting, by British artist Alfred Duke, shows a pack of hunting beagles picking up the scent and creating a noisy clamor. These bold, strong, intelligent dogs may have an ancient origin. The Norman French used them for pursuing hares – they were so small that they were carried in saddle-bags or the pockets of mounted hunters.

SWIMMING DOG
This golden retriever has been told to fetch a stick out of the water, but it would collect a dead animal killed in a hunt just as quickly. Most dogs enjoy a swim, but retrievers are specially bred to bring back birds and other animals that have been shot and have fallen into the water. These dogs are trained to respond quickly to commands. They have a "soft" mouth, which means they can carry a dead bird in their mouths without biting into it. Their fur has a very thick, water-resistant undercoat.

DIANA THE HUNTRESS
This enamel painting on a metal plaque from Limoges shows what hunting hounds looked like in France in the mid-16th century. The picture is of Diana, the Roman goddess of the hunt. There are many legends about Diana, who shunned the society of men and was attended always by a large number of nymphs. In classical art she was often shown in a chariot drawn by two white stags.

All dogs swim by paddling with their front legs, just as children do when they are learning to swim by "dog-paddling"

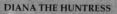

Herding dogs and sheepdogs

LASSIE
The rough collie got a new name from the *Lassie* films.

THE USE OF DOGS TO PROTECT and herd livestock dates from as early as 1000 B.C., when farmers began to breed large numbers of sheep, goats, and cattle. In his book on raising farm animals, in the first century A.D., the Roman writer Columella noted that shepherds preferred white sheepdogs because they could be distinguished from wolves. There was always a danger that the shepherd would kill his own dog, believing it to be a wolf that was about to kill his animals. Even today, although the wolf is nearly extinct, most of the many varieties of herding dogs that are bred in nearly every country of the world are light-colored or tan and have a lot of white in their coats.

OLD DOG'S TAIL
Old English sheepdogs are seldom born without tails, and most puppies have their tails docked (pp. 44–45) for showing. A heavy sheepdog without a tail is not much use because it cannot run fast. Although called "Old," this breed is probably not of ancient origin. In this 19th-century English painting, the sheepdog is ready to tend its sheep.

ROUGH COLLIE
The original rough collie was the traditional sheepdog of the lowlands of Scotland, and probably took its name from the "colley," or local black sheep. For hundreds of years it was an essential partner for every shepherd. Today, the rough collie is one of the world's most popular breeds and has become a successful show and companion dog.

Straight, muscular forelegs and powerful, sinewy hindlegs enabled the rough collie to cover great distances while herding sheep

Long-haired, thick coat is usually pale gold, tan, and white, with dark hair around the head

BELGIAN SHEPHERD DOG
There were no wolves left in Belgium when the shepherd dogs of this country were first developed as distinct breeds in the 1880s. Therefore they, and indeed the modern German shepherd, are an exception to the tradition that herding dogs should be light-colored.

ROUND-UP TIME
The Border collie, originally from the border country between England and Scotland, is one of the finest sheepdogs in the world. It is bred as a working dog, not for showing.

DOGS DOWN UNDER
The Australian cattle dog is now the official name for this breed of strong working dog, developed by cattlemen in the 1830s. It has had a number of previous names, such as the Queensland blue heeler. These dogs round up cattle by nipping at their heels.

A SHEPHERD AND HIS DOG
Both this Rumanian shepherd and his dog are well prepared for the rigors of the winters in central Europe. These traditional breeds – of both sheepdog and shepherd – are heavily built, have thick coats, and are excellent guardians of the flock.

IMPASSE
Englishman Thomas Bewick (1753–1828) was famous for his animal engravings. Here a dog teases a bull.

The ears should be semi-erect with the tips pointing forward

SMALL BUT BEAUTIFUL
Domestic animals on the Shetland Islands, off the northern coast of Scotland, tend to be small. This is because the climate is cold and windy, and food is often scarce. So small animals, such as the Shetland pony and Shetland breed of cattle, survive better in the tough conditions than larger animals that need more food. The Shetland sheepdog, or shelty, is also a successful product of breeding for small size. A tiny version of the Scottish rough collie, it was the traditional herding dog of the Shetland Islands.

The shelty's sharp sense of smell can seek out and save a lamb that is buried in the snow

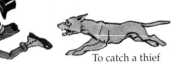

Helper dogs

To catch a thief

DOGS OF WAR
The intense loyalty of dogs to people means that they can be trained to carry out missions under conditions of great danger.

Dogs have been indispensable throughout history as helpers in human societies. Besides being used to herd other animals, and for companionship, their principal function has been to guard the home and the farm. Today the job of the guard dog has broadened and includes protecting factories and industrial estates. To shut up a dog on its own in an empty building or other enclosed space and expect it to live by itself, and to ward off intruders, goes against all the social behavioral patterns of the dog, and is cruel. Dogs that are trained by the police for protection and for detection of drugs and explosives are seldom alone and usually live well-balanced lives. Certain breeds are more naturally aggressive than others, but nearly all dogs have to be specially trained to be aggressive to strangers and not to their handlers. Today there are innumerable ways in which dogs help the sick, the disabled, and the lonely – and by insisting on a daily walk they help keep their owners healthy.

Strong teeth and a sturdy jaw – with the lower jaw projecting above the upper – help the boxer to keep strangers at bay

Boxers have great strength and energy – the powerful forequarters are inherited from the bulldog

Thick black and tan coat is long and wavy and provides perfect protection against the intense cold of the Swiss mountains

BERNESE MOUNTAIN DOG
In the old days the large mastiff-type dogs in Switzerland were used for protecting merchants, cattle traders, drovers, and their herds as they traveled through the mountain passes. Until the early 1900s they were all known simply as Swiss mountain dogs, but today there are four separate breeds – the Bernese (pp. 56–57) from the province, or canton, of Berne; the Appenzell from the canton of the same name; the Entlebuch from the canton of Lucerne; and the Greater Swiss.

DOGS IN SPACE
Sending dogs into space may have contributed greatly to human knowledge, but for the dogs it must have been a terrifying experience – no different from any other laboratory experiment. The first dog to be sent into space was the Russian dog Laika in 1957.

St. Bernard to the rescue

БЕЛКА и СТРЕЛКА

RESCUE DOGS
For several hundred years, dogs bred at the monastery of the Great St. Bernard Pass in Switzerland were trained to rescue travelers lost in the mountains.

A DOG WITH THREE HEADS
In ancient mythology, Cerberus was a three-headed dog that stood at the gates of hell, to prevent the living from entering and the dead from leaving.

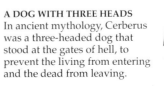

German shepherds have plenty of room in their straight, wolflike jaws for strong, healthy teeth

SEEING EYE DOGS

Most people know that dogs can be trained to be "the eyes" of people who are blind. They can also learn to hear for the deaf, be a helping hand to disabled people, and provide companionship to the old, the sick, and the deprived.

Cutting the ears to make them permanently erect (cropping) is illegal in Britain, but it is done in other countries to make the dog look fiercer

Cutting off the tail (docking) is a painful procedure and prevents the dog from expressing its natural behavior

This Doberman pinscher is warning an intruder not to come any closer

THE FIERCE DOBERMAN

The Doberman pinscher is a born guard dog and has been bred to be aggressive. But like nearly all dogs, when correctly reared, it can also be an affectionate companion. The breed was first developed in Germany at the end of the 19th century.

GOOD COMPANIONS

Both the boxer and the German shepherd (pp. 10–11) are guard dogs and were first bred in Germany. The boxer is of mastiff origin (pp. 34–35) crossed with the bulldog (pp. 54–55). The German shepherd is a droving or herding dog that has become the most popular guardian and protector of property worldwide. Dogs of both breeds are also loyal and affectionate companions for people if reared and trained correctly, but they need plenty of space and exercise.

The powerful hindquarters make the German shepherd a good jumper and able to cover great distances without getting tired

BRAVE GUARD DOG

As long as this dog can spend most of its time with a person, it will be content and can be trained to protect and guard people and buildings.

Dogs in sports

OVER THE AGES, people have used dogs as entertainment in a great variety of sports, many of which have unfortunately involved much cruelty. In Roman times, dogfighting and "baiting" became fashionable sports and continued until the late 1800s. Baiting was a sport in which people released a pack of dogs in a ring with another animal, such as a bear or bull (pp. 54–55), and watched as the animal was torn to death by the dogs. Although these inhumane activities are now illegal, they are still practiced in some places. Dogs like to compete with each other, however, and there are many sports that are not as cruel. The large number of different breeds of sight hounds (pp. 14–15) have all been developed for coursing, or chasing after, fast-running prey such as hares. They were often used – together with birds of prey – in the sport of falconry. In northern Africa and Asia, both the Saluki and the Afghan hound (pp. 48–49) were bred for chasing gazelles. Today, in greyhound racing, dogs are bred for speed, and run after a mechanical "hare."

GOING TO THE DOGS
Greyhounds and whippets are the number-one choice around the world as racing dogs. Here, though, the greyhound is used for advertising Camembert cheese.

"THE DOG FIGHT"
The spectators in this painting, by English artist Thomas Rowlandson (1756–1827), are urging their dogs to fight and are betting on which dog will win. Today this cruel sport is illegal in the U.S. and many other countries.

Keen sight of the borzoi (pp. 14–15) will help it to win a race – or, as in former times, to hunt well

MUZZLED
Dogs get very excited when they are racing, so usually they wear muzzles to keep them from biting other dogs during a race.

Borzoi

Deep chest and freely swinging shoulders enable the dog to take long strides

Long, muscular lower legs

Well-feathered tail is long, set low, and gently curved

Well-muscled legs make the Saluki a powerful runner

THE ROYAL SALUKI

The Saluki is one of the oldest breeds of sight hound (pp. 14–15) in the world, and dogs of this type can be seen in the tomb paintings of ancient Egyptian pharaohs. For thousands of years Salukis have been bred by Arab peoples for chasing gazelles and, together with falcons, for killing large birds, such as vultures.

AWAY TO THE RACES

Although dogs have been used in the Arctic for hundreds of years to draw sleds (pp. 56–57), today they have been mostly replaced by mechanical snowmobiles. However, within recent years, the sport of sled racing over long distances with huskies has become very popular – especially in Alaska.

TINTIN AND SNOWY

These popular cartoon characters race over the snow with their trusty team of huskies.

Dense, curly ruff on neck

Long, wavy, silky hair is usually white with splotchy dark markings

Ankle joint, or hock, is high on the leg, which makes the leg very long and powerful

THE HARE AND THE DOG

The use of greyhounds for hare coursing – pursuing game with dogs that follow by sight, not scent – is probably one of the most ancient of all sports.

BEAUTIFUL BOUNDER

The borzoi comes from Russia and used to be called the Russian wolfhound because it was used by the aristocracy for hunting and chasing wolves. The borzoi may have been developed from long-legged sight hounds (pp. 14–15), such as the Saluki, which were then crossed with long-haired, local, collie-type dogs. They were bred to look as aristocratic and beautiful as possible to match the noble aspirations of the Russian emperors.

Hounds

Hounds are one of the most easily recognizable group of dogs, as they all have similar features – floppy ears, long muzzles, and powerful jaws. They are strong and hardy – even the more delicate-looking breeds – and are relentless hunters. Hounds hunt either by smell, like the bloodhound, or by sight, like the greyhound and Afghan hound. Sight hounds (pp. 14–15) have lightly built bodies, are fast runners, and are used in the hunt to chase prey. Scent hounds (pp. 16–17) are slower and more heavily built, and are used to sniff out prey; their long, droopy ears help guide the smells from the ground to the nose. Hounds vary in size more than any other dog group. The Irish wolfhound, a sight hound originally used for hunting wolves, is the heaviest of all dogs; the miniature dachshund, a scent hound used for hunting badgers, is one of the smallest. Many breeds of hound are still used today for hunting, but others, such as the wolfhound, are house dogs and companions. The lifespan of small hounds is around 15 years, but very large hounds live on average for only about half this time.

ELEGANT BORZOI
The borzoi (pp. 14–15) is the most aristocratic of all hounds, and it looks as though it would hardly deign to behave like an ordinary dog.

WELSH LEGEND
The town of Beddgelert in Wales is named after the famous deerhound Gelert, killed by Prince Llewellyn after he thought the dog had killed his child. The prince found blood all around the baby's cradle so he killed the dog with his sword. But then he found the baby safe, and nearby a dead wolf, killed by his faithful dog. This Welsh legend is one of several similar stories known in many countries around the world.

LONG-HAIRED BEAUTY
The Afghan hound is an ancient breed of long-haired greyhound that originated in Afghanistan, where it was used by the royal family for hunting gazelle (small antelope). After its arrival in Britain in the early 1900s, this dog was bred to be even longer-haired and more silky. The Afghan hound is a popular show dog but retains its hunting and racing instincts.

Wrinkled brow and face

Short hair on face and along the back

Long, silky ears

"Dewlap," or loose folds of skin hanging beneath its throat

Very long, silky hair

TALLYHO
The foxhound has changed little since medieval times; it is still used today for fox hunting. Foxhounds do not make good house dogs because for centuries they have been bred specifically for hunting and for living close together in large numbers as a pack.

A DIGNIFIED DOG
In modern times the role of the bloodhound has been that of a guard dog rather than a hunting hound, but its fearsome reputation as a relentless tracker has survived in legend if not in fact. Breeding for show standards has led to the folds of skin around its head becoming over-developed, and this can lead to health problems.

THE HOUND OF THE BASKERVILLES
Shown above is a still from one of three film versions of British writer Sir Arthur Conan Doyle's (1859–1930) famous Sherlock Holmes story.

Tail is carried erect, not curled forward

THE GREAT DOG OF IRELAND
The ancient breed of hounds used in Ireland since medieval times for hunting wolves probably died out completely in the 19th century – more than 100 years after the last wolf was killed in Ireland. A British army officer recreated the breed in the late 1800s, and since then the Irish wolfhound has become a giant. It is the tallest dog in the world, with a shoulder height of up to 3 ft (94 cm). However, the old Irish wolfhound looked more like a rough-haired greyhound.

HUNTING HARE
The beagle was originally bred for tracking hares in Britain and France, but it is now very popular in the U.S. and Canada, where it is used for hunting cottontail rabbits. Because they are small, have a uniform weight, and tolerate living together in large numbers, the beagle has become the breed most frequently used for laboratory research.

A DEVONSHIRE HUNTING TAPESTRY
This detail, from one of four Flemish tapestries woven in the early 1400s, shows a medieval hunting scene with richly dressed ladies and noblemen, their hounds, and prey of boar. These tapestries were once owned by the Duke of Devonshire in England.

DON'T BADGER ME!
Dachshund means "badger dog" in German. This breed was originally an "earth dog" – a terrier used to dig out badgers from their dens. Because "hund" was translated into English as "hound," these dogs became classed in that group. The miniature dachshund is a popular house dog, weighing up to 12 lb (5.5 kg).

Straight, strong forelegs and long, muscular hindlegs enabled the Irish wolfhound to cover great distances in chasing its prey

The dachshund can have three varieties of coat – short-haired, long-haired, or, as here, wire-haired

49

Sporting dogs

SPANIELS, SETTERS, pointers, and retrievers all fall within the category of dogs called "sporting dogs." Today, sporting dogs are mostly used to help hunters shoot game birds. For example, pointers and setters use their sharp eyes and keen noses to find the game. Then they point their body toward the bird and freeze, to guide the hunter. Sporting dogs must also have "soft" mouths so that they can fetch, or retrieve, the dead or wounded prey undamaged by their teeth (pp. 40–41). These breeds are not usually aggressive, having been originally bred to live together in kennels. They respond very well to training – for this reason they are raised not only for sport but also as house dogs and companions. The Labrador retriever is probably the most popular animal companion and helper dog (pp. 44–45) in the world.

READY, AIM, FIRE
Above all else, the hunter's dog must not be afraid of the noise of a gun.

English setter holds a stick in its mouth, in the same way as it would a bird

An object for training a sporting dog to become used to holding prey in its mouth

English setter's thick coat enables it to hunt in winter and to endure the cold weather

AT THE END OF THE DAY
Along with their hunting dogs (pp. 40–41) and a horse, these hunters, wearing hacking jackets and riding breeches and holding their guns, are at rest after a long day's hunt.

BRINGING HOME A BIRD
The retriever is trained to retrieve (bring back to the hunter) game after it has been shot.

Setters and pointers often hold up one front foot as they "freeze" into position before the shoot

RED-HAIRED BEAUTY
The Irish, or red, setter has a silky coat and a gentle nature. However, the red setter is a high-strung and headstrong breed, and it is often considered to be unreliable as a sporting dog.

A REAL CHARMER
Although it is now a show dog and pet, the cocker spaniel was bred as a sporting dog and got its name from its ability to flush out birds called woodcocks.

Muscular, strong-boned legs helped the cocker to be an excellent bird dog

A DAMP DAY FOR DUCK HUNTING
Duck shooting often ends up with both the hunter and his dog getting very wet. Spaniels, which have been bred for hundreds of years as water dogs, are the traditional companions of the duck hunter. This painting (above) shows a Chesapeake retriever, a curly-coated retriever, and an Irish water spaniel (from left to right).

GETTING THE POINT
Pointers are trained to "point" (pp. 16–17) at hidden game with their noses. This makes them essential companions on bird shoots.

Dog made of Italian glass decorates lid of Austrian box, c.1800

Tail is called "feathered" when it looks like the feathers of a bird

GOOD SHOT
This 18th-century tile from France shows a hunter – wearing a shoulder pouch for collecting the game – and his dogs chasing the prey, which is probably a rabbit or a hare.

SETTING UP THE GAME
The English setter is one of the oldest breeds of sporting dogs. Originally, the setter was a spaniel that was trained to "set" the game – to go into bushes to scare, or spring, birds into the air so that they could be killed. In the Middle Ages birds were caught in nets; later they were shot with guns. This setter is holding a stick in its mouth in the same way that it would hold a dead bird.

Special long lead allows sporting dogs to escape their leash quickly

Terriers

The tip of the Airedale's small, V-shaped ear falls forward to the top of its eye

TARTAN TERRIER
The modern Scottish terrier, or "Scottie," is descended from short-legged, rough-coated working terriers that were bred for centuries in the Scottish Highlands. The Scottie was not typically black until the 1900s.

Terriers are known as "earth dogs"– *terra* means "the earth" in Latin. They are great diggers and need no encouragement to go down holes in the ground in pursuit of burrowing animals such as foxes, rabbits, and rats. Terriers have an ancient history in Britain and have always been used as sporting and hunting dogs. They are the best dogs for killing rats on farms and in mines. Traditionally, many types of terriers have been bred in various regions of Britain – like the Border, Scottish, and Yorkshire terriers – but a few other countries have also developed new breeds, such as the Australian terrier.
Many of the terriers registered by the kennel clubs of today have been distinguished as separate breeds only in the last hundred years.

Strong teeth and vicelike jaws prevent prey from escaping

Coat is stiff and wiry and lies close to the body; it requires careful grooming (pp. 62–63)

Long, strong jaws help the Australian terrier catch rabbits, rats, and even snakes

A SHAGGY DOG STORY
Early British immigrants to Australia took their dogs with them, and by the early 1900s this new breed – the Australian terrier – had been developed from a mix of cairn, Dandie Dinmont, Irish, Scottish, and Yorkshire terriers.

A ROMAN DOG
Discovered in northern England during the 1800s, this copper alloy figure (made between the first and fourth centuries A.D.) looks like an old terrier breed – the Aberdeen.

The ears of the low-slung, compact Norfolk terrier are slightly rounded at the tip and drop forward close to its cheek

Given a rubber ring or ball, the playful nature of a terrier is quite apparent

A GIANT AMONG TERRIERS

The Airedale terrier is named after the district in Yorkshire, England, where it originated. The largest of all terriers, it was developed in the mid-1800s by crossbreeding (pp. 60–61) the now-extinct black and tan terrier with the otterhound to increase its size and strength for the hunting of large prey. The Airedale was also used in World War I as a messenger dog (pp. 44–45).

Tail is set high and carried erect, not curved forward over its back

A LEGEND IN HIS OWN LIFETIME

When a gentleman named Greyfriars died in Edinburgh, Scotland, his faithful little dog – a Skye-type terrier called Bobby – refused to leave his master's grave until he himself died, ten years later. So the legend of "Greyfriars' Bobby" began.

DECORATED "DRUMMER" DOG

Dogs have always been popular as mascots. Shown here is the brave war hero, Drummer, the mascot of an English army regiment, the Northumberland Fusiliers. Drummer's death was reported in a British newspaper in 1902.

FOXY FELLOW

In the late 1800s, the fox terrier was the most popular breed of dog in England. Today this popularity has been taken over by the smaller Jack Russell terrier (pp. 38–39). Fox terriers can be either wire-haired like this one, or smooth-haired.

With excellent balance, a wire-haired fox terrier is ready for action – whether tearing up a carpet or hunting foxes (pp. 28–29)

Bedlington's long ears, pear-shaped head, and curly, light-colored coat make it look more like a lamb

LIKE A LAMB

All sorts of breeds, including the whippet, otterhound, and bull terrier are thought to have contributed to the development of the Bedlington terrier, at one time known as the Rothbury terrier.

DANDIFIED DOG

Dogs have been used in advertising for a long time. Here, a terrier in his finery graces a magazine cover.

DIGGER BONES

The Norfolk terrier is a new breed that is descended from terriers bred in East Anglia, England. It is an active little dog with short legs and a wiry coat. This terrier used to be called a Norwich terrier, which had both prick, and drop-eared varieties, but in 1965 the name of Norfolk was given to those with drop ears.

Terriers – like this Norfolk – dig with both their front and hind legs

Nonsporting dogs

NONSPORTING DOGS is a miscellaneous collection of dogs that includes the ones left over after all the other breeds have been neatly categorized into the other five groups (pp. 48–53, 56–59). The title of "special dogs" might be more apt to describe the range of individual, and special, characteristics, as this group includes some of the more unusual dogs. The history of some nonsporting dogs goes back for many centuries – the forerunner of the chow chow was first bred 3,000 years ago in Mongolia, Asia, for use in war, and later, in China, as a source of fur and food. In fact, most of the dogs in this group were originally bred for work or sport but are now kept primarily as pets and show dogs. For example, at one time French hunters sent poodles to retrieve ducks; bulldogs were once bred for baiting bulls (pp. 46–47); and Dalmatians were used for herding cattle and hunting game. This group also includes national dogs from various countries – the Boston terrier from the United States, the bulldog from Britain, and the poodle from France.

MADE IN AMERICA
The Boston terrier is a very popular dog and is one of the few breeds to have been developed in the U.S.

USEFUL HELPERS
In this detail from a 17th-century Japanese screen, a richly dressed Portuguese merchant is shown with his servants and faithful companion – his dog.

The back has retained the powerful muscles of the old-fashioned bulldog

BAT-EARED BULLDOG
In the old days French bulldogs were used for baiting donkeys (pp. 46–47). Today they are smaller and live more peaceful lives, but it is still a tough breed and a good guard dog.

Legs are set wide apart, allowing the dog to stand its ground

French bulldog

CHINESE CHOW
The breed of chow chow is now 200 years old, having been developed from a pair of dogs of pariah origin (pp. 36–37) introduced into England from Canton in southeast China in the 1780s. English naturalist Gilbert White (1720–1793) in his *Natural History and Antiquities of Selborne* (1789) described the dogs as "such as are fattened in that country for the purpose of being eaten."

Very thick fur and curled tails are typical of spitz dogs, like the chow chow, for adapting to sub-Arctic temperatures

The tongue of the chow chow is always blue-black, an unusual characteristic inherited from the dog's Chinese ancestors

THE BEST OF BRITISH
The bulldog is the national symbol of the British, portraying strength and stubbornness. This breed was developed for baiting bulls – setting dogs on bulls for public sport – and dates back to at least the 16th century.

JUMPING THROUGH HOOPS
Because the poodle is one of the most easily trained of breeds, it has been commonly used as a circus dog. In this fine gold brooch, made in Austria c.1890, a clown encourages his troop of dogs to perform tricks.

THE ELEGANT "COACH DOG"
In the 1800s, it was very fashionable in England and France to have a "coach dog" to accompany the carriages of aristocrats. The horses' harness and dog's coat colors were coordinated.

Muzzle is adorned by a massive mustache

This strongest of all the schnauzers – the giant schnauzer – stands up to 2 ft (65 cm) at the shoulder

BUSHY-HAIRED BEAUTY
Schnauzers got their name from the German word *Schnauze*, meaning "muzzle." Originally used for herding sheep in southern Germany, nowadays these energetic dogs make excellent companions and family pets. In the U.S. and Canada the giant and standard schnauzers are classified as working dogs (pp. 56–57), and the miniature is in the terrier group (pp. 52–53).

The Dalmatian's coat is always pure white with distinctive black or brown (liver) spots

SPOTTED DOG
There are several legends about the origin of Dalmatians. Some people believe that these dogs came from India with gypsies who settled in Dalmatia, now Yugoslavia; others think that the breed originated in Italy. Dalmatians were first brought to England by travelers to Europe in the 18th century. It then became fashionable to have these aristocratic-looking dogs running beside the carriage horses of gentlemen. The Dalmatian is unique in that it excretes urea, and not uric acid, in its urine. This means that it should be a popular breed with gardeners because its urine does not kill lawn grass.

Legs are long and built for speed and endurance

PRETTY AS A PICTURE
Poodles were first bred as sporting dogs (pp. 50–51), probably in Germany, but their intelligence and attractive appearance soon led to their chief role of much-loved house dog. An early form of the pet poodle as it was in the 1700s is shown in this painting by Jean Jacques Bachelier (1724–1806).

Working dogs

SUPERIOR SWIMMER
The huge Newfoundland breed may originate from Pyrenean mountain rescue dogs taken to Newfoundland in eastern Canada by Spanish fishermen.

ROYAL CORGI
Since medieval times in Wales there have been short-legged cattle dogs, called corgis, that are now favorites of British royalty.

THE EARLIEST DOMESTIC DOGS (pp. 34–35) were companions to human hunters in their pursuit of all sorts of animals from mammoths to small birds. Over the thousands of years since that time, dogs have always worked with people. Before Europeans reached North America in the 15th century A.D., the dog was the only animal that had been domesticated by American Indians. The primary work of these dogs was to draw a travois, or sled, laden with possessions when a family moved from place to place. They were also used to help in the great bison hunts when a whole herd of bison could be driven to its death. Eskimo dogs and huskies have been indispensable in polar exploration. In Europe, where there have been horses and oxen for pulling carts, dogs have not been as commonly used for this type of work. For the purposes of dog shows, the breed registry includes herding dogs (pp. 42–43) and helper dogs (pp. 44–45) in the category of working dogs.

AGILE AUSSIE
The job of the Australian kelpie is to round up sheep that have strayed from the main flock – it has the odd ability of running along sheep's backs to reach the head of the flock. A well-trained dog can do the work of six men, and it is able to travel 40 miles (64 km) in a day.

Color of a husky's eyes can be brown or blue – or even one of each

Siberian husky

Dogs lose heat through their tongues, which is why they pant to cool down – even in the Arctic

Thick ruff of fur around neck and stocky shape keep as much warmth as possible inside the husky's body

SWISS BLANKET
The Bernese mountain dog, a typical helper dog (pp. 44–45), is an example of many breeds of mastiff-type dogs that have been used throughout Europe and Asia since the Roman period for guarding and protecting travelers in the mountains. By sleeping beside the traveler at night, the dog's exceptionally thick fur would keep both human and animal warm, and by day the dog would be able to follow the path with its nose, even through thick snow.

SPECIAL DELIVERY
In Switzerland and other very mountainous countries, mastiff-type dogs were the best animals for drawing milk carts steadily along narrow paths. From the earliest times (pp. 34–35), the mastiff's natural aggression made it an excellent guard dog.

IN THE GREAT FAR NORTH
The word "Eskimo" means "snow." It is no longer used for the Inuit and other native North Americans who live in the Arctic regions, but the name has remained in use for their dogs.

The Great Dane, like all mastiffs, has a very deep and powerful chest

The working dog's harness is designed to give it the greatest pulling power

WHEN IS A DANE NOT A DANE?
The Great Dane was developed in Germany, where in the old days no castle was complete without a pair of these giant mastiff-type dogs to guard it.

The tail trails when the dog is working or at rest, but curves over its back when the dog is running

HARNESSING A HUSKY
The Siberian husky is the only pure breed of this dog. Otherwise, the name is used in North America, particularly Canada, for all the dogs of the spitz type that are used for drawing sleds and for hunting seals and other Arctic animals. Peoples who have lived for thousands of years in the Arctic zones of North America, Europe, and Asia could not have survived without their working huskies and Eskimo dogs (pp. 46–47).

HERALDIC DOG
Images of dogs have often appeared in heraldry. This husky is an important part of the coat of arms for Canada's Yukon Territory.

Toy dogs

THE CATEGORY OF TOY DOGS INCLUDES all the smallest show breeds. Most dogs in this group have a height of less than 12 in (30.5 cm). Perhaps one of the most remarkable facts of all about the domestication of animals is that even every toy dog, however small, is descended from the wolf. Because, genetically, it has inherited the same characteristics as its wild ancestor, even the tiniest dog will try its best to behave like a wolf. It will gnaw at bones, guard its territory, and show its feelings to other dogs with its posture and tail – just as a wolf does. The Romans were probably the first to breed miniature dogs, and bones of dogs that are as small as any of today's breeds have been found on Roman excavations. The small white dogs known as Maltese (pp. 10–11) are probably of Roman origin, and dogs of this type often appear in Roman paintings. Other tiny dogs have been bred since ancient times in Tibet, China, and Japan. In Europe, toy spaniels were the favorite companions of the aristocracy throughout the Middle Ages.

Dismal Desmond
– a popular stuffed toy
from the 1930s in England
– lives up to his name

*Small, V-shaped
ears set high
on head*

*Fine, silky-textured
coat is long except
on face and ears*

DOG'S DINNER
In a detail from this charming, 19th-century French painting, entitled *Caninemania*, the family pet is treated as a very special dinner guest – to the exclusion of the lady's friend who has been relegated to a seat in the corner – and is, therefore, out of the picture.

*Large, broad head
with flat profile
and snub nose*

TOY TERRIER TERROR
The Australian silky terrier is not a toy by nature. This short-legged, compact dog can kill a rat or a rabbit in seconds, and it is claimed to be equally quick at killing snakes. Although it looks a little like a Yorkshire terrier, this breed is reputed to have originated entirely by crossbreeding in Australia.

CHINESE LION DOG
Another name for the Pekingese is the "lion dog of Peking." There is a legend that these dogs were first bred to represent the lion spirit of Buddha. Today the Pekingese, with its big eyes, round head, flat face, and soft fur looks more like a cuddly toy than a lion.

*A Pekingese
walks with a side-
to-side rolling gait,
trying to distribute its
weight evenly on its
short legs*

PEKINGESE PAIR
Miniature dogs have existed in China for at least 2,500 years, but the Pekingese itself is probably not a very ancient breed. The Pekingese was kept as a palace dog by the Imperial family of Peking (now Beijing). It was introduced to the West by English forces who looted the Imperial Palace in 1860; since that time the breed has become smaller and more short-legged.

A POPULAR PINSCHER
The miniature pinscher is a much older breed than its larger cousin, the Doberman pinscher. As with the Doberman, show standards specify that the tail of the breed must be docked (pp. 44–45), a practice that prevents the dog from expressing its emotions naturally and upsets its balance when running.

Head is well rounded with a turned-up nose

PAINTED POMERANIAN
In the 18th century, when English artist Thomas Gainsborough (1727–1788) painted this Pomeranian mother with her puppy, the breed was much larger than it is today. The Pomeranian is a miniature spitz and has the stocky body, pricked ears, ruff of fur, and curled tail that is typical of this group of northern dogs (pp. 46–47).

ROYAL FAVORITE
Probably originating in China or Japan, this good-tempered little dog arrived in England from France in the 16th century. It was Charles II's great fondness for this dog that gave the breed its name.

The tail of the Bichon is always curled over its back

The miniature pinscher is no softy and has the strong legs of a much larger dog

King Charles spaniel

BICHON FRISE
Within recent years the Bichon Frise (meaning "curly lap-dog") has become increasingly popular, especially in the U.S. The Bichon is a Franco-Belgian breed, much like a small poodle, and though it looks, literally, like a toy, it is a lively, playful little dog.

The white coat has a very soft woolly underfur and an upper layer of loosely curled silky hairs

Crossbred dogs

T HE DEVELOPMENT OF BREEDS OF DOG for different purposes, such as hunting (pp. 40–41), herding (pp. 42–43), guarding (pp. 44–45), and sport (pp. 46–47), has been a long, slow process that has continued over more than 5,000 years. However, most of the dogs in the world are still mongrels, or crossbred dogs. These are dogs that have interbred with each other at random, as opposed to purebred dogs (pp. 48–59), which are dogs of the same breed that have been selectively bred by humans. It is possible for all 400 breeds of dogs in the world to interbreed, because they are all descended from the wolf (pp. 8–9) and, therefore, they all belong to one species. It would obviously be difficult, from a practical point of view, for a Great Dane to mate with a tiny Pekingese. However, many unlikely crosses have occurred – such as a dachshund with a German shepherd. It is often claimed that crossbred dogs are more intelligent than purebred dogs, but it is more likely that their behavior just shows more variation because they combine good characteristics of a number of different breeds.

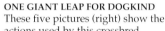

SITTING DOG
This mongrel is eagerly waiting for its reward.

ONE GIANT LEAP FOR DOGKIND
These five pictures (right) show the actions used by this crossbred dog in jumping over an obstacle. The tail is particularly important for keeping the dog's balance.

Tail arched upward helps dog retain its balance

Strong, well-muscled legs help this dog jump high off the ground at the beginning of its leap

Correct stance for getting ready to take off

GOOD DOG!
Training a dog to establish good behavior patterns can be a long and arduous process, as this child realizes – but both will get their rewards in the end.

"HIS MASTER'S VOICE"
This painting by English artist Francis Barraud (1856–1924) was bought by the British gramophone company EMI for $180. The dog, "Nipper," was the artist's own, and he was a crossbreed with a lot of bull terrier in him. This charming picture and its slogan were first registered as a trademark in 1910, and are still known in the U.S. as a sign of RCA records.

ON THE DOGHOUSE
Snoopy – the world's favorite cartoon dog – is mainly a beagle with a bit of something else too. Many amusing adventures befall him each week in comic strips, but – like most dogs – he likes to sleep and dream, especially on top of his doghouse.

Strong, well-proportioned legs

DOGS' BEST FRIEND
This poignant painting, entitled *L'Ami des Bêtes*, by French artist Constantin Magnier, was published in 1910. It shows an old tramp sharing his small amount of food with his only friends – a large group of mongrels.

WAITING FOR A FRIEND
A dog's wagging tail is seen as a friendly gesture toward either humans or other animals. This small figure of a pet dog, made of terra cotta in 500 B.C., was found in Boeotia, in central Greece.

Alert ears

Eyes looking straight ahead

Mouth open for more air

KEEPING ITS COOL
This crossbred puppy (pp. 20–21) is licking its nose to help keep cool on a hot summer's day.

Tail arches over back when dog touches down

Bright, alert eyes

Medium-length coat – neither too short, nor too long

Well-defined body outline

Front legs are straight and feet firmly on the ground when jump is completed

Well-shaped nose

Pert, expressive ears

A MOTLEY CREW
These crossbred dogs are without any extremes of physical form or function, and they will provide companionship, friendship, and loyalty for their owners. Aside from their individual endearing qualities, crossbreeds are often tougher, better-tempered, less disease-prone, and more adaptable than their pedigree counterparts.

Caring for a dog

Ownership of a dog should be taken on only by people who are prepared to keep the animal for the whole of its life – up to 17 years. For the first year, training a puppy is not very different from bringing up a child, and in some ways it is much easier, as a dog can be housebroken much faster than a child can be potty-trained. The dog's every need must be attended to, but at the same time it must be taught to take its place within its human family. A dog should never be left on its own for more than a few hours. It requires clean drinking water, regular meals at set times, and hard biscuits or bones to chew on, to keep its teeth clean. Every dog should be treated for internal and external parasites, such as tapeworms and fleas, and inoculated against diseases such as distemper and, in countries where it occurs, rabies.

BATHTIME FOR BONZO
This little girl is intent on keeping her pet clean.

2. A partially clipped poodle

3. Fine-tuning underneath

TICKLISH TAPERING
Originally the poodle was a water dog (pp. 54–55), and its coat was clipped to keep it from getting matted. Today, most poodles are companion animals, but even so the coat should be clipped for the dog's comfort rather than for show standards.

4. Very wet poodle after its bath

5. Perfecting the tail

6. The end result

Bowl of water
at all times

Dish of dry,
crunchy dog food

In the same way that a
wild wolf will have its
own den, every domes-
tic dog needs a bed of
its own. This can be a
basket, or a beanbag,
or an old armchair that
the dog has taken over
for itself.

Assortment of
dog biscuits

Favorite toys

Rawhide bone

Brush and comb

Lead

Collar

*Dense coat of a
poodle needs extra-
special grooming*

Essential aids for looking after a dog

Cleaning
the teeth

Clipping
the claws

Trimming
hair
between
the claws

STRAY DOGS
The most frightening event that can happen to
a dog is to be lost or abandoned by its owner.
If the lost dog is taken to a home for stray
dogs, it will become extremely anxious and
confused. A dog should never be turned out
onto the street. If it can no longer be kept, nor
a new home found for it, as a last resort the
kindest thing to do is to have it put to sleep by
a veterinary surgeon.

THE WINNER IS
Dog shows have been held for the last
hundred years. The exhibition of dogs at
shows keeps up the standards of the breeds
and allows all the people concerned to meet
and discuss their achievements and problems.
However, the points of the breeds as set for
showing are not always in the dog's best
interests – for example docking the tail
(pp. 44–45) removes a most important means
of communication for the dog, as well as
upsetting its balance when it runs.

NAME............ TEL.......
ADDRESS
....

IDENTIFICATION
Every dog must carry its
owner's name and address.
This can be engraved on a
tag attached to the dog's
collar, or it can be as a code
in a small tattoo, or by a tiny
coded pellet under the skin.

Did you know?

AMAZING FACTS

Dogs can smell and hear better than they can see. Dogs see things first by their movement, second by their brightness, and third by their shape.

Rhodesian ridgebacks have a visible ridge, which is made up of forward-growing hairs running along the top of their back.

A dog's sense of smell is at least a thousand times better than ours. "Scent" dogs, which have been bred to pursue other animals by their smell alone, can distinguish several different scents at the same time, and identify them as well. Dogs have 20 to 25 times more smell-receptor cells than people do.

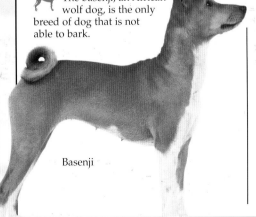

A bitch suckling her young

Hair from some dogs, such as the Samoyed, can be spun into thread and woven into clothes.

Dogs hear much better than humans do. Dogs can hear high-pitched sounds that humans are not aware of at all. They can also hear sounds from a great distance, and can work out the location of a faint sound.

The basenji, an African wolf dog, is the only breed of dog that is not able to bark.

Basenji

Dogs eat quickly and can regurgitate food very easily. This is useful for wolves, who are able to travel a long way from a kill back to their dens, where they regurgitate the food to feed their pups. It is also useful for other dogs, who get rid of bad food by throwing it up.

Long-faced dogs have eyes on the sides of their head, and so have a wider field of vision. Short-faced dogs tend to have eyes that are facing forward, and so are very good at judging distances.

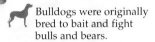

Big dogs tend to have larger litters than small dogs, but small dogs usually live longer than large dogs.

Bulldogs were originally bred to bait and fight bulls and bears.

Dogs only have about 10 vocal sounds, whereas domestic cats have about 20. Dogs communicate a great deal through body language—young puppies understand hand signals before words in early training.

Almost one in three families in the United States and France owns a dog, whereas in Germany and Switzerland there is only one dog for every 10 households.

On average there are 320 bones in a dog's skeleton, but the exact number depends on the length of the dog's tail.

A dog was the first animal to go into space. In 1957, Russian scientists sent Laika, a small dog, around the earth in a satellite.

The greyhound is one of the oldest breeds of dog.

A Newfoundland dog swimming

Newfoundland dogs are strong and agile swimmers. Like many breeds of dog, they have webbing between their toes, which helps them paddle through water.

A newborn puppy is deaf for two to three weeks until its ear canals open up.

Most puppies have 28 temporary teeth, which they begin to lose at about 12 weeks of age. They have usually grown their 42 permanent teeth by the time they are six months old.

Unlike cats, dogs cannot retract (pull in) their claws.

Bloodhounds have an amazing sense of smell. They can successfully follow scent trails that are more than four days old.

Bloodhound

64

A dog searching a car for drugs

Record Breakers

THE OLDEST DOG
An Australian cattle dog named Bluey lived to be 29 years and five months old.

THE HEAVIEST AND LONGEST DOG EVER RECORDED
An Old English mastiff named Zorba holds the record as the heaviest and longest dog. In 1989, Zorba weighed 343 lb (155 kg) and was 8 ft 3 in (2.5 m) long from nose to tail.

THE TALLEST BREEDS AND THE SMALLEST BREED
The smallest breed of dog is the chihuahua. However, dogs from a number of breeds can attain 36 in (90 cm) at the shoulder, and so several are classed as the tallest breeds. They are the Great Dane, the Irish wolfhound, the St. Bernard, the English mastiff, the borzoi, and the Anatolian karabash.

Great Dane

Q Why do the police use dogs?

A The police use dogs because of their excellent sense of smell. "Sniffer" dogs sometimes help the police to track down escaped prisoners, and also help to find illegal drugs.

Q Why do dogs chase their tails?

A A puppy instinctively chases the tip of its tail, perhaps because it resembles moving prey. If an adult dog chases its tail it is more likely to be because it has not had enough exercise, or because it has fleas, or some other medical problem.

Q Which dogs are considered the smartest?

A Most sheepdog breeds are very intelligent and easy to train. Sporting dogs also respond well to training. Some of the smaller breeds, such as the poodle, are very good at performing tricks.

Q How should you approach a strange dog?

A If you have to get close to an unfamiliar dog, kneel down and let the dog come and sniff the back of your hand. Do not make sudden movements or stare into the dog's eyes, as that might feel like a threat. If the dog seems aggressive, avoid eye contact and back away slowly. Do not turn and run, as that might encourage the dog to chase you.

Q Why do dogs pant?

A Unlike people, dogs cannot cool themselves by perspiring. They only have sweat glands in their feet, and these don't have a great effect on their body temperature. But panting helps a dog stay cool. When saliva evaporates from the tongue and mouth, it helps to reduce the dog's body heat.

Q Why do dogs eat grass?

A Dogs often eat grass when they are not feeling well. The grass makes them throw up, after which dogs may feel better.

Border collies often herd sheep

Q Can dogs see in color?

A A dog's color vision is limited to shades of gray and blue. The colors green, red, yellow, and orange all look the same.

Q Why do dogs' eyes glow in the dark?

A At the back of each eye a layer of cells called the "tapetum lucidum" reflects light back into the eye, making it possible for the dog to see in dim light. When a bright light strikes a dog's eyes it is reflected back, making the eyes appear to glow.

Q What is a dorgi?

A When a dachshund and a corgi mate, their offspring are called dorgis. Famous dorgis include those born to England's Queen Elizabeth's corgi and the Queen Mother's dachshund.

Identifying dogs

Dogs come in many different sizes—from the tiny chihuahua to the giant Irish wolfhound. The American Kennel Club recognizes 150 breeds of dog and divides them into seven groups, according to the use for which the breed was originally developed.

HEAD SHAPES

Long-headed dogs have long, often tapering noses. Round-headed breeds have a short nose. Square-headed dogs have a step between the muzzle and the forehead. It is known as the "stop."

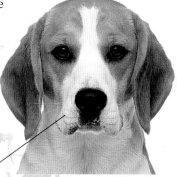

A beagle has a square muzzle.

The borzoi has long, powerful jaws.

A pug has a very flat face.

Square head   Rounded head   Long head

COAT TYPES

Short-haired dogs have a smooth coat. Most long-haired breeds have a thick undercoat with a longer coat on top. Wire-haired dogs have a short undercoat with longer, wiry hairs on top. A few breeds have a corded, felt-like coat.

Long-haired Old English sheepdog

Short-haired Entelbuch mountain dog

Wire-haired schnauzer

Hungarian puli

Greyhounds have excellent vision.

Racing greyhounds wear a coat showing their number.

HOUNDS
For a long time, people have bred dogs to help catch other animals. Some extremely fast hounds, such as the greyhound, whippet, or saluki, are "sight" hounds, which means that they chase things that they can see. Other hounds, such as bloodhounds, beagles, and bassets have great stamina and pursue by scent rather than by sight.

Dalmatian puppies are colored pure white when they are born; their spots develop as they grow.

NON-SPORTING DOGS
This group contains a wide variety of different dogs, bred for specific functions not included in the working or sporting categories. Japanese noblemen bred the akita, for example, to help them hunt bears, wild boar, and deer. Nowadays the akita is used mainly as a guard dog. The Dalmatian was a carriage dog—it trotted along between the back wheels of a carriage in order to put off any potential attackers.

The Jack Russell terrier's coat is mainly white.

TERRIERS

Terriers are alert, bold, and fearless. Most were originally farm dogs, kept as rat catchers. They love digging, and some, such as the fox terrier, were used to flush out foxes. Others, such as the Airedale terrier, hunted badgers and otters.

HERDING DOGS

Many dogs in this group still herd sheep and cattle today. The border collie is excellent with sheep, while the blue heeler can accurately control cattle. Herding dogs are active and intelligent. Most have a double coat, which protects them in rough weather conditions.

Chihuahua

SPORTING DOGS

Gun dogs are responsive, friendly, and highly intelligent, but require a great deal of exercise. The group includes pointers, spaniels, setters, and retrievers, like this Labrador retriever. Many are good at flushing out birds for hunters and at retrieving the bird once shot. Some, such as the épagneul Picard, are particularly good at retrieving water-birds, while the Spanish water dog is excellent at retrieving game from the sea.

TOY DOGS

Known also as companion dogs, breeds in this group are usually friendly and intelligent and love attention. Most are also small in size.

WORKING DOGS

This group includes guard dogs, such as the mastiff and Doberman, dogs to pull sleds or carts, such as the Siberian husky and the Bernese mountain dog, dogs for helping fishermen, such as the Newfoundland dog, and dogs for search and rescue, such as the St. Bernard.

Find out more

ONE OF THE BEST WAYS TO FIND OUT MORE about dogs is to spend time with them. You could offer to walk a neighbor's dog, or simply spend some time with friends who have a dog. You could go to one of the many different dog shows that take place throughout the year, and watch the competitions and training displays. Or you might consider volunteering to help the Humane Society or the ASPCA. Charities welcome the help of volunteers as they work to rescue and find homes for injured and abandoned dogs and puppies.

Tell your puppy immediately if it has done something wrong.

DOG TRAINING
The Canine Good Citizen Program (CGC) is a national certification program begun in 1989 to reward dogs that have demonstrated good manners. CGC is a two-part program to develop responsible pet owners and well-mannered dogs. Dogs are tested by trained evaluators in the community and at most dog shows.

A dog must learn to sit obediently at its owner's heels.

A PET PUPPY
If you get a puppy as a pet, it is important that you spend enough time with it while it is young. Dogs relate best to people if they start having plenty of contact as young puppies. Your dog needs clear instructions on how to behave, but also plenty of support, affection, and praise.

CRUFTS
The largest dog show in the world, Crufts takes place over four days in March each year, and has more than 120,000 visitors. Hundreds of stands promote all the things you might need for your pet, and there are many competitions and displays. More than 20,000 top pedigree dogs compete for the sought-after award of "Best in Show."

Crufts
BEST IN SHOW
Pedigree

Crufts
RESERVE BEST IN

HELP DOGS IN TROUBLE

Consider helping the Humane Society and American Society for the Prevention of Cruelty to Animals (ASPCA), either with your time or by raising funds. Both charities rescue animals that are abandoned or badly treated and find new homes for them.

An ASPCA officer comforts a scared dog.

The assistance dog provides warmth and affection as well as practical help.

HELPFUL DOGS

Well-trained dogs can be a huge help to people who are physically disabled. The dogs open and close doors, pick up things that have been dropped, turn lights on and off, go for help, and provide constant love and companionship. Find out more about charities such as Paws with a Cause or Dogs for the Deaf to see how you can help.

AGILE DOGS

By going to dog shows you will find out a lot more about what dogs can do. Some shows include agility competitions, in which dogs jump fences, weave through poles, cross see-saws, and go through tunnels, as well as jumping onto tables and lying immobile for a few seconds before continuing. Owners run around the course directing their dog. The winner is the fastest dog with the fewest penalties for knocking down fences or missing parts of the course.

Places to Visit

WESTMINSTER KENNEL DOG SHOW
New York, New York
• The second longest running sports event in the United States (behind the Kentucky Derby) the show is held each year in February at Madison Garden in New York. The show features more than 2,500 dogs from 162 breeds competing to be chosen "Best in Show." For the exact dates and more details go to: www.westminsterkennelclub.org

NATIONAL DOG SHOW
Philadelphia, Pennsylvania
• Hosted by the Kennel Club of Philadelphia, this televised show presents more than 2,500 dogs competing for Breed, Group, and "Best in Show" honors.

THE AMERICAN KENNEL CLUB MUSEUM OF THE DOG
West St. Louis County, Missouri
• One of the world's finest collections of art devoted to the dog, including paintings, drawings, sculptures, and decorative art pieces.

LEEDS CASTLE
Kent, England
• The castle exhibits an interesting collection of dog collars through the ages.

A dog collar from the collection at Leeds Castle

USEFUL WEB SITES

◆ For details about the American Kennel Club and its many activities:
www.akc.org

• For full coverage of the Westminster Dog Show go to
www.westminsterkennelclub.org

• To find a dog trainer in your area see:
animalbehaviorcounselors.org/

• For information about dog breeds:
www.yourpurebredpuppy.com/dogbreeds/

• For information about the Humane Society or adopting a pet:
www.hsus.org

• To find out about adopting a pet from the ASPCA or for advice about caring for your pet:
www.aspca.org

• Paws with a Cause trains assistance dogs for people with disabilities. Find out more at:
www.pawswithacause.org/

• For information about caring for your pet, breeds, training, and shelters:
www.aboutdogsonline.com/

St. Bernard

Glossary

BAIT Something edible put out to attract animals

BAT EARS Erect ears that are wide at the base, rounded at the tips, and pointed out

BITCH An adult female dog

BREED A group of dogs with particular characteristics. Humans control breeding to achieve specific features, such as coat type or head shape. If the breeding is not strictly supervised, characteristics can very quickly be lost.

BREEDING The process of producing animals by mating one animal with another

BREED STANDARD The official description of a breed, setting out size, weight, color, etc.

BRINDLE A mix of tan and black hair.

An Italian greyhound bitch with her puppies

BRUSH A term used to describe a bushy tail; also a fox's tail

CAMOUFLAGE The coloration of an animal that either blends in with the color of the surroundings or breaks up the animal's outline with stripes or spots, making it harder to see. Camouflage can be important both for animals that hunt and for those that are hunted.

CANID A member of the dog family. The term comes from *canis*, which is the Latin word for dog.

CANINE Dog or doglike; also the large tooth between the incisors and the premolars, used for gripping prey

CARNIVORE A member of the order Carnivora—which contains animals that have teeth specialized for biting and shearing flesh. Most carnivores live primarily on meat.

Beagles have drop ears.

CLASS Any of the taxonomic groups into which a phylum is divided. A class contains one or more orders. Dogs are part of the class Mammalia.

CROP The removal of the top of the ears so that they stand upright, and are pointed rather than rounded at the tip

CROSSBRED An animal whose parents are from different breeds, or are themselves crossbreds

DEN The retreat or resting place of a wild animal

DEW CLAW The claw on the inside of the legs. It is not used for any particular purpose.

DEWLAP The loose folds of skin hanging under a dog's throat, as in the bloodhound

DOCK To remove an animal's tail, or part of it, by cutting

DOG Specifically an adult male dog, but used in a general way for all dogs, regardless of age or sex

DOGGY PADDLING To swim moving your limbs in vertical circles, the way that a dog swims

DOMINANT The animal that is stronger and in a more powerful position in a group

DOUBLE COAT A coat made up of a soft, insulating undercoat through which longer guard hairs protrude

DROP EARS Ears that hang down, close to the sides of the head

ECOLOGICAL NICHE The position occupied by a plant or animal within its community, including all the ways in which it interacts with living and non-living things

ERECT Standing upright

FAMILY Any of the taxonomic groups into which an order is divided. A family contains one or more genera. Canidae is the name of the dog family.

FERAL DOGS Domestic dogs that have returned to living in the wild and now live totally outside human control

FORELEGS The front legs of a four-legged animal

GENUS (plural **GENERA**) Any of the taxonomic groups into which a family is divided. A genus contains one or more species.

GROOM To brush, clean, and style a dog

GUARD HAIRS The coarse hairs that form the outer coat of some mammals

HACKLES The hair on the back and neck, which is raised when a dog is frightened or in order to show aggression

HINDLEGS The back legs of a four-legged animal

HOUNDS A group of dogs used for hunting, including fast but lightly built "sight" hounds, and stocky but relentless "scent" hounds.

Labradors are sporting dogs

JAWS The part of the skull that frames the mouth and holds the teeth

LIGAMENT The tough tissue that connects bones and cartilage and supports muscle.

LITTER A group of puppies born at one time to one female

MONGREL A dog of mixed or unknown breeding. Also known as a cross-breed.

MOLT To lose hair so that new growth can take place. Dogs molt particularly in the spring when they lose the thick coat they grew for the winter.

Three crossbred dogs, or mongrels

MUSCLE Tissue that can contract or relax and as a result allow movement

MUZZLE The part of the head that is in front of the eyes.

NON-SPORTING DOGS A varied range of different dogs that are useful to humans in one way or another

OLFACTORY Relating to the sense of smell

ORDER Any of the taxonomic groups into which a class is divided. An order contains one or more families. Dogs belong to the order Carnivora.

PACK A group of animals of the same kind. The animals usually live together, may be related, and hunt cooperatively.

PEDIGREE The record of a purebred dog's ancestors

PHYLUM A major taxonomic division of living organisms. A phylum contains one or more classes. Dogs belong to the phylum Chordata, which includes animals that have backbones (known as vertebrates).

PUPPY A dog that is less than one year old

PUREBRED A dog whose parents belong to the same breed. Also known as a pedigree dog.

REGURGITATE To bring up food that has been eaten. Wolves and other hunting dogs do this to feed their young.

RUFF Long, thick hair around the neck

SADDLE Black markings in the shape and position of the saddle on a horse

SCALE OF DOMINANCE The order from the most powerful to the least powerful animal in a group

SCAVENGER An animal that feeds on other animal remains that it steals or finds

SCENT HOUND A dog that has been bred to use its excellent sense of smell more than its sight or hearing when pursuing other animals. Bloodhounds, beagles, and foxhounds are scent hounds.

SIGHT HOUND A dog with excellent sight that will chase game while it can see it. Greyhounds, Afghan hounds, and borzoi are sight hounds.

SKELETON The framework of bones that gives shape to an animal, provides anchorage for muscles, protects vital organs, is a source of blood cells, and provides a mineral store

SPECIES Any of the taxonomic groups into which a genus is divided. Members of the same species are able to breed with each other.

SPITZ Any of various breeds of dog characterized by a stocky build, a curled tail, a pointed muzzle, and erect ears. The chow chow is a spitz.

SPORTING DOGS A group of dogs trained to work with a hunter or gamekeeper at pointing, flushing out, and retrieving game

STEREOSCOPIC VISION The ability to see a slightly different picture with each eye, and, by putting them together, to judge distances accurately

STUDBOOK The book in which breeders register the pedigrees of dogs

SUCKLE To suck milk from the mother. The term also means to give milk to a young animal.

TAPETUM LUCIDUM The cells at the back of a dog's eye that reflect light. The tapetum lucidum makes it possible for a dog to see well when there is not a lot of light.

TAXONOMIC Relating to the classification of organisms into groups, based on their similarities or origin

TENDON A band of tough tissue that attaches a muscle to a bone

TERRIERS A group of active, inquisitive dogs originally trained to hunt animals living underground

THIRD EYELID Situated inside the upper and lower eyelids, a thin fold of skin that can be drawn across the eye, protecting it from dust and dirt

TICKED A coat in which spots of color stand out against the background color

Yorkshire terrier

TOY DOGS A group of very small dogs popular as pets

UNDERCOAT (or **UNDERFUR**) The dense, soft fur beneath the outer, coarser fur in some mammals

WEAN To cause a puppy to replace its mother's milk with other food

WHELP A puppy that has not yet been weaned and is still feeding on its mother's milk. The term also means to give birth to puppies.

WORKING DOGS A group of dogs that work for people, for example, by pulling sleds, herding sheep, or guarding buildings

Puppies playing

Index

Acknowledgments

The publisher would like to thank:
Trevor Smith's Animal World, V Battarby, R Hills, E Mustoe, H Neave, D Peach, R Ramphul, S Renton, S Surrell, J Williamson, and J Young for lending dogs for photography.
The zoos of Augsburg, Duisburg, and Osnabrück for providing wild dogs for photography.
J Larner for grooming section.
The British Kennel Club and Mrs R Wilford for breed information.
The Natural History Museum's staff and R Loverance of the British Museum for their research help.
J Gulliver for her help in the initial stages of the book.
C Carez, B Crowley, C Gillard, T Keenes, and E Sephton for their editorial/design assistance.
J Parker for the index.
Illustrations:
E Sephton, J Kaiser-Atcherley
Picture credits
The publisher would like to thank the following for their kind permission to reproduce their photographs:

a=above t=top b=bottom c=center l=left r=right
Advertising Archives: 60bl, 63bl
Allsport: 46cl; /Bob Martin: 15cr
American Museum of Natural/ A E Anderson: 9tl; /Logan: 9ct
Ancient Art and Architecture Collection: 49bcl
Animal Photography/Sally Anne Thompson: 39tr, 45tr, 45br, 50c
Ardea, London Ltd/Eric Dragesco: 25tl; /Ian Beames: 35br; /John Daniels 68c, 69bl; /Jean-Paul Ferrero: 22t, 37cl, 56c; /Kenneth W Fink: 20bl, 31br; /M Krishnan: 36cbl; /S Meyers: 28tl
Australian Overseas Information Service, London: 37tr
Bridgeman Art Library: 6tl, 6–7t, 7tr, 40cl, 41tl, 41tr, 42tr; Cadogan Gallery, London: 18cl; Oldham Art Gallery, Lancs: 46tr; Rafael Valls Gallery, London: 55bl
British Museum: 34tl, 34br, 35cl, 35bl;
Museum of Mankind: 26br
Jean-Loup Charmet: 19bl, 51bl, 58cr, 61tr
Bruce Coleman/John M Burnley: 19tl; /Jessica Ehlers: 36bl; /Jeff Foott: 32cl; /Gullivan & Rogers: 33br; /F Jorge: 32tr; /Leonard Lee Rue: 25tc, 29tl
Columbia Pictures Television: 39tl
Corbis: 64–65 (background) /Gallo Images 25crb /Richard Hamilton Smith 67b /Kevin R Morris 67tr /Tom Nebbia 64tr, 69c /Rick Price 66–67 (background) /Ariel Skelley 68tr /Greg Smith 65tl

/Dale C Spartas 67cl
Syvia Cordaiy Photo Library: 63cbr
Cyanamid (UK)/Animal Health Div: 11b
C M Dixon: 36tl
DK Images: Tracy Morgan 64bl, 65cr, 66clb, 66bl, 66cbl, 67tl, 68–69 (background), 70t, 70cl, 70b, 70–71 (background)
EMI Records: 60cr
English Heritage/Keith Hobbs: 52cr
e.t. Archive: 48bl
Mary Evans Picture Library: back jacket cl, 10tl, 16bl, 21c, 22cb, 44bl, 47bl, 48tl, 48tr, 53tc
Marc Henrie, ASC (London): 42br
© Hergé: 47cr
Michael Holford: front jacket br, 4br, 34bl, 38cl, 58bl
Hutchison Library/H R Dörig: 32tl; /R Ian Lloyd: 35tl
ILN Picture Library: 53cl, 56br
Image Bank: 12tl, 30tl
Imperial War Museum: 44tr
Kennel Club Picture Library: 68b
Dave King: 10br, 13ctl, 39 br, 42 bl, 45cr, 48cl, 51tl, 52tl, 52–53tl, 53c, 54tr, 54bl, 57tl, 61bl
Kobal Collection: 42tl; /Avco Embassy: 23br; /Twentieth Century Fox: 49tl
Michael Leach: 29cr
Leeds Castle: 35bc, 69cr
Macmillan Inc: 8br
National Archive of Canada/

Karen E Bailey (C–137830): 57b
National Portrait Gallery: 56tr
Natural History Museum Pubs: 9br
Peter Newark's Pictures: 25c, 29cr
NHPA/Michael Leach: 36ctl; /Mandal Raijit: 27bl
Robert Opie Collection: 44tl, 50tl, 54cr, 62tl
Oxford Scientific Films/O Newman: 23cr
Planet Earth Pictures/J R Bracegirdle: 24bc; /Jim Brandenburg: 11cr, 23bl; /J Scott: 21tl
Axel Poignant Archive: 36br
Retrograph Archive/Martin Breese: 14tr, 20tl, 42cl, 44br, 46tl, 50cl, 53cr
Reuters /Andy Muller 66cr
RSPCA Photolibrary /Paul Herrmann: 69tl
Gary Santry: 61cr
Science Photo Library/John Sanford: 8tl
South American Pictures/Tony Morrison: 33bl
Tate Gallery: 59tr
Tring Museum: 7bl
© 1990 United Feature Syndicate, Inc: 60br
F R Valla: 35cr
V & A Museum: 29br, 56tl, 58tl
Werner Forman Archive: 23cr, 24tr, 41tc, 54tl
Zefa Picture Library: 47cl
© Dr Erik Zimen: 18ctr, 19tr, 21cl, 23tr
Cover images: Front: B: Monica Dalmasso/Getty, b; Swim Ink/Corbis, tl.
All other images © Dorling Kindersley